PETULANT

How Pre-Feminist Peevishness and

Guerrilla Warfare Has Poisoned

Political Points of View

Cover design by the author.

DISCLAIMER:

The author has no intention to slight, defame, or offend any person living or dead and apologizes for any factual errors that may unwittingly be presented in these pages.

Several of the examples given in this book are fictional in order not to slant the reader against one side of the political aisle or another. The memes are real and were all taken from the Internet in 2020.

PETULANT

Table of Contents

The stronger you feel,
the easier it is
to convince someone
you are right
(even if you are wrong).

TONY ANNESI
PETULANT
HOW PRE-FEMINIST PEEVISHNESS
AND GUERRILLA WARFARE
HAS POISONED
POLITICAL POINTS OF VIEW

Introduction

The Inspiration of Frustration

MR. POIRIER'S VOCABULARY

When you walked into Mr. Poirier's tenth grade English class in 1962, you immediately looked up to the right corner of the chalkboard to see five vocabulary words listed there—a different five every day. Your job was to write them down and learn the definitions for Friday's vocabulary quiz, twenty words that petould, week-by-week, add up to 200 over ten quizzes and would count toward to total grade at the end of the term.

As a dutiful student and one who planned to get A's in English, since it was the subject I intended for my college major, I made sure I looked up each meaning and studied them every day, even asking my mother (from whom I seldom asked help for anything) to quiz me on them.

She was cooperative and probably happy to help since I usually shrugged off any of her attempts to advise or especially to cajole me into acting in my own self-interest (at least according to her view of my self-interest). I always felt smothered and simply wanted to be on my own, even though I knew I was three years away from going off to college and at least seven years from moving out of the house altogether.

She took particular delight in quizzing me on the word "petulant", letting me know that she felt it defined me. While pointing my way, she said, "That's you!" I understand how she could have thought so. For her, I was peevish, moody, irritable, testy, and touchy. She was probably right, from her point of view. From my point of view, I never saw her trying to avoid the things that got me annoyed so easily. To be frank, I was intelligent enough to know better, but not mature enough to see her point of view. And to be fair, she was nearly thirty years older than I and had the same difficulty understanding my point of view. Ironically, she was being petulant about my petulance.

My ace-ing nearly every vocabulary quiz was like an objective verification that my way of running my life, at least in the academic department, was justified. I don't know if my petulance at home helped my achievements, but I used that simple empirical data to offer evidence that I generally knew what I was doing and did not need help from anyone. (Ironically, I was able to ignore the relevant fact that it was my mother's aid in reviewing vocabulary every evening, that helped produced that empirical data, thus proving to my more mature self that cherry-picked empirical data does not tell the whole tale.)

We always seemed to have a contentious relationship as if she were never going to give up her gut feeling about what was right for me and I was never going to give up using empirical evidence to argue that I could make my own decisions. If that sounds reminiscent of the current political culture, you understand why I've used this little vignette to open this book.

ANOTHER SORT OF PETULANCE TO CONSIDER

In that same high school, one of Mr. Poirier's friends was our tenth grade science teacher, Mr. Ligor. If you will excuse my portraying a single point of view as if it were fact: every one of his students liked Mr. Poirier while none liked

Mr. Ligor. Even the guys who played football on his Junior Varsity squad did not think highly of him. Both he and Mr. Poirier were obviously intelligent, and both tried to be fair—even strict when necessary. But somehow Poirier earned our respect when he was tough while Ligor never did.

If I were to guess the reason (guessing is all I can do since, even if psycho-social analysis were my field of expertise, it is awfully difficult to perform decades after the fact)—but, if I were to guess why Mr. Ligor was so disliked, I would say it was because he tried too hard to be "the good teacher" while Mr. Poirier already knew he was a good teacher and just let his skills flow naturally. In other words, our fourteen- and fifteen-year-old brains picked up on the idea that Ligor was tightrope-walking while Poirier had long before built a wide and sturdy suspension bridge. The result was, at least in my considered opinion over the years, that Mr. Ligor displayed an overt petulance either when we students did not cooperate with his desires in class or when his learned methods to cope with our unruly and hormonally-challenged teenaged nature did not yield the results he expected.

PETULANCE LINKED TO GUERRILLA WARFARE

One time we were making too many puns and other comments during one of Mr. Ligor's classes and, after having sent several culprits to the office over the last few weeks, he finally decided to demand that our entire class report to his classroom immediately after school for a detention of an unstated duration. This seemed colossally unfair to most of us since the majority of the class had not misbehaved. What was worse was that Carla, a co-captain of the field hockey team, was to have an away-game that afternoon and Mr. Ligor, a coach himself, was aware of it. When she was overly fidgety in her chair, glancing frequently at the clock over the door, Mr. Ligor addressed her directly: "If you think you're going to make that field hockey game, forget it." Carla, never given to emotional outbursts, broke down in tears.

I don't remember if Carla had participated in the earlier class disturbance, but even if she had, this seemed to be cruel and unusual punishment, especially coming from a coach. Had he shown a little leniency to Carla, telling her she could make up the time another day, he might have won our respect, but as far as I was concerned (and I'd be willing to wager that this was true of many of the other students), his action that day had sealed his fate. Oh, henceforth we might fool around less frequently in class (thus giving him a Pyrrhic victory), but he would never get our respect or voluntary cooperation. We were the outwardly respectful but inward resisting guerrillas who could not win, but who would be damned if they did not spit in their ruler's soup. Because we, as students, were not allowed to reason with his authority, we reacted emotionally. When the annual Science Fair came around, Mr. Ligor had difficulty finding any student that wanted to exhibit anything. A good exhibit would have made him look better to the public and to the administration than we felt he deserved. Soup spat in.

PRE-FEMINIST GIRLS MAKING THEIR OWN DECISIONS

Although different sources use different dates, we can approximate the first wave of feminism as a period between the late nineteenth century and 1920. The second wave occurred from the 1960s to the 1980s. Many have suggested two more waves: a third wave between 1980 and 2000, and a fourth contemporary wave. I was in high school in the early 1960s, so I know the girls in my school were aware of bra-burnings and the movement not to shave underarms and legs. We all seemed to tacitly accept the concept of equal pay for equal work since it was as incontestable as was equal treatment under the law in The Civil Rights Movement, but I did not notice any of the girls flaunting a burning desire to imitate "feminist" actions, go unshaven, or publicly demonstrate for equal rights.

My female high school classmates were not the activists like those with whom I attended university, but to be fair, neither Vietnam nor the birth control pill were overwhelming the news as yet. Nevertheless, this large group of pre-feminist girls were not "too feminine" to speak up for themselves, nor did their femininity prevent them from achieving. Achieve they did. In fact, I was the only boy in our Honor Society.

Why do I mention this prior-to-feminism group? You might think I am trying to create a justification for not needing a feminist movement, but that is not the case. Rather, in calling the high school girls I knew "pre-feminists", I mean to say that they were prepped for the feminism of the late 1960s *as well as* having been socially indoctrinated in the female wiles of women that came before them. I could posit a pre-1960 (year the birth control pill was approved for oral use) feminine attitude, and then a post-1960 feminist attitude, but neither history nor attitudes divide so neatly. Rather, in high school, I saw both old-school female roles being played out and new-school female roles being accepted without resistance from either girls or boys.

We had a strong girls' sports department in our high school as well as a couple of women teachers who could bench press some of the boys, so no one tested them in the same way we had tested Mr. Ligor. Still, Salli and Dianne were not above using old-school tactics to get what they wanted. Salli and I argued all the time, admittedly half-seriously, half humorously, but nevertheless frequently enough so it was clear I would not be asking her to the prom. (As it turned out, Salli became Queen of the Prom while Dianne, my date, was one of the three "princesses".)

One weekday evening while I was doing homework on my mother's dining room table, the phone rang. It was Salli. Now, Salli had never called me for any reason in the six years that I had known her. She said that Dianne and she were alone in her house doing an assignment together, were having difficulty, and wondered if I could help. I can't remember if the assignment was math, history, or English, but in any case, I was more than surprised. Dianne was a high achiever, a member of the Honor Society, and someone I would not have expected to ask for assistance. Salli would have asked for help, to be sure, but only from Dianne or another of her girlfriends. Even more shocking was that she suggested that I drive to her house, only two miles away, in order to help in person.

Obviously this was suspicious. On one hand, Salli could not be suggesting anything romantic since Dianne was there, but on the other hand, inviting me to help two of the most attractive girls in my class when Salli's parents were not around was clearly an invitation that only a pre-feminist manipulator of men (or a teenaged boy in this case) would consider.

I drove, I arrived, I helped, I was thanked, and then off I went. There was nothing romantic, nothing suggestive, nothing that portended a new wrinkle on our future interactions—just a lure dangled and seized. Then, the fish was thrown back into the water. A feminist woman would never have done such a thing. She would either have asked for help outright or, more likely, would have refused help from anyone of my gender.

These girls were in-between being dependent and independent—not feminists yet (and still willing to use their sexuality to get what they wanted), yet doing it as a last resort. They had been duplicitous, which rendered me feeling both appreciated and used. In fact, I was unsure that Salli had not simply been proving to Dianne that she could manipulate me.

This little story is not to make a judgment about feminism, but to make a parallel between this sort of middle-of-the-road pre-feminism and today's political discourse. Either one side or the other will imply their intentions, only to reveal that they were not *really* their intentions once those intentions were realized. In politics, it is often called moving the goalposts, or when outright honest, it is called deception.

AN UNREALISTIC BUT HELPFUL CATEGORIZATION

Let's pretend there was a change in culture in 1960. No, not the cultural upheaval of The Civil Rights Movement, Feminism, the sexual revolution, or Vietnam, but a non-existent, purely theoretical change in a majority of women from not being socially equal to men to suddenly being completely equal.

In this fantasy timeline, pre-1960s wives and girl-friends, when frustrated, would sometimes lash out against their male counterparts, but since they did not have the physical power or social standing to be directly effective, they created ways to influence and manipulate the allegedly dominant male into seeing things their way.

Equally fanciful is that, after 1960, all women became feminists and feminists received everything they were seeking, thus they no longer needed to influence or manipulate anyone. In this whimsical scenario, they could and actually did, argue like their male counterparts. This artificial categorization allows us to type a sort of "pre-feminist" argumentation style, not always sneaky like guerrilla warfare, but like guerrilla warfare, stemming from a desire to win at any cost.

Chapter 1.

Examples of Petulant Argumentation

I have survived numerous relationships, many with really fine women that I was happy to have known and others with women who, it seemed to me, had issues. I am not sure if their issues were with men, as such, or if other issues impinged upon them so that they released upon their closest male companion that which relationship specialist Alison Armstrong calls "the rage monster". Rage monsters do not respond to logic. In fact, they are insulted by logic because logic may provide a reason for them to control their emotions, something they need to let flow if they are to return, as some future point, to normality (albeit with bared trigger fingers sensitive to the stimuli that released the monster in the first place).

Compiled from decades of observation, the following is a list of the way pre-feminist women would express their disagreement with a man, at least in my experience. I suspect they used these methods in dealing with women, as well, but other women are familiar with the tactics so these petulant argumentative attempts are often less successful.

- Taking something out of context
- All accidents or coincidences will be interpreted as if they had been intended
- Misquoting/intentionally misinterpreting
- Exaggerating the alleged problem
- Taking one aspect of what you say and completing the narrative with their own implications
- Jump to extreme conclusions/actions
- Mind reading
- Drawing conclusions based on facts that could have other interpretations
- Assuming that the opposite party means something they may not mean
- Looking for anything that justifies a biased narrative

- Dwelling on what the other side *doesn't* do, rather than evaluating what it does
- Attempting to "win" (or have the other party give in) rather than find the objective truth
- Never taking the blame for anything/never admitting she is wrong
- Assuming that "since I know I am virtuous, you cannot be".

Some of this can be seen as temporary narcissism, perhaps compensation for feeling undervalued. Some of it can be seen as applied tactics coming from feeling un-powerful.

PRE-FEMINIST WOMEN AS GUERRILLAS

For a moment, let's draw that line that I mentioned could not really be drawn. Let's say that pre-1960, women acted one way, while post-1960, they acted another. Not accurate, I admit, but simplifying the timeline will make my argument clearer. It will also show that my contention is not actually about women, but about method.

Let's further assume (equally inaccurately) that, between 1960 and 1980, the women's movement achieved all its goals of equality. Let's assume that post-1980 women now held positions that only men held before 1960, and no longer were considered merely second-class citizens, tagging along with their male counterparts. Having made these simplistic assumptions, how would we assume women acted in the old pre-1960s days when they felt they were not treated in the way that men were. Would it not be logical to assume that they were feeling, like my 10th grade science class, that although they may have misbehaved once in a while, by-and-large, they were not treated with respect? Would they not feel that they had to grin and bear it too often? Would they not feel that they should develop methods by which to influence their "oppressors"? Would they not act somewhat like guerrillas—like resistance fighters in an occupied country?

HOW GUERRILLA WARFARE HAS POISONED POLITICAL POINTS OF VIEW

Vince Lombardi famously said, "Winning isn't everything. It's the only thing." As I asked in *10 Guideline Principles*, did Lombardi mean that he would be willing to cheat in order to win? I doubt it, and yet modern political theorists can use his quote as if it were an American justification for guerrilla warfare.

Guerrilla warfare in Vietnam gave many people the inspiration to "fight dirty" politically since they saw political victory as more important than fairness. They thus sacrificed the long-term cultural value of fairness for sort-term political wins. This trade off is the key element in understanding the motivations of political actors, and those motivations are the keys to understanding their tactics. Much of their tactical efforts are intended to change minds through a less-than-logical, more-or-less emotional, often self-centered method of argumentation that portrays itself as self-denying and other-oriented.

Would Americans (or citizens of other countries, for that matter) tolerate their Olympic rivals drugging their amateur athletes to gain an advantage? No, Americans (and citizens of other countries) do not even tolerate a *professional* athlete's use of performance enhancing drugs. I am not saying that drugging is not done; rather, I am saying that an athlete can ruin his/her entire career if someone discovers that his/her personal skills are enhanced artificially and illegally. Why? Because fans want a level playing field.

Most of us want the rules of engagement to be understood and adhered-to. And yet we also realize that real life is not sports. In real life, there will be those who don't care about the rules. Just as actual street fighting is not rule-bound as is the Mixed Martial Arts you see on TV, there are those who plan to win politically and are willing to evade or outright ignore any prearranged war conventions to do so. Those who want to win no matter the cost, use guerrilla tactics.

A resistance movement that defends its own country from invasion does not care to use fair play, but at least it attacks the invaders' armed forces. Guerrillas that want to win political dominance, however, will take advantage of the generally decent behavior of innocents they choose to hate, attacking civilians, and hiding behind other civilians to do so. An example of this is when Palestinian movements fire mortar shells and rockets into Israel while stationed on the tops of school buildings so that Israel cannot ethically return fire on those stations. They consider themselves guerrillas and resistance fighters, while Israel and other nations consider them terrorists. In either case, they intentional avoid any conventions of war. The Geneva Conventions came about because people wanted some rules of engagement during wartime. The idea of a "war criminal" came about so that those who ignored those war conventions would be punished. When have we last seen a guerrilla action that would not qualify as a "war criminal" action?

Now in the USA, politics has become closer to war than to sports. Politics has never been totally clean—even Adams and Jefferson planted stories about each other while running for office. Although the Left and the Right have been disagreeing since at least the founding of the Democratic and Republican parties, once elections were over, they often returned to a relationship in which both sides cooperated for the good of the country as a whole, or at least engaged in negotiations so that one side would get a bit of what it wanted in order for the other side to advance the agenda it wanted. Always? No, of course not. There were several periods in which the contention bordered on rage, and rage is one step south of war. Although contention and even nastiness was undeniable, also undeniable was idea that "the good of the country" would be a unifying goal, and the U.S. Constitution would provide the rules of engagement.

One party cannot unilaterally change The Constitution. In fact, *both* parties acting together cannot do so. A change to The Constitution requires a constitutional convention and then a vote in which three quarters of the states (38 of the current 50) ratify any amendment that the convention proposes. The founding fathers obviously wanted a solid, stable set of rules that different political points of view would have to acknowledge and accept.

Is there a way to change laws and governmental behaviors that could make Americans willing to ignore or downplay the validity of The Constitution? Over the decades, several have been tried. The dominant methods have been as follows:

- Since The Supreme Court interprets The Constitution, attempts have been made to change the number of justices on that court so that there would be more justices who favor one point of view over another;

• Presidents have attempted to appoint judges that have more loyalty to a political point of view than the Constitutional rule book;

• Scholars have written articles that reinterpret the traditional understanding of The Constitution;

• Intellectuals have attempted to convince a key number of senators and congressmen/-women that The Constitution needs to be seen as constantly adjusting to the times;

• Members of congress have made laws that take liberties with a traditional interpretation of that document, hoping they will not be challenged; and

• Intellectuals, scholars, media policy wonks, and politicians have attempted to convince the voting populace that a certain end goal is more important that the Constitutional rules of engagement.

It is this last method that has now adopted tactics historically used by "pre-feminist" women who felt un-powerful. If they did not have the power to control parts of the culture, or at least the power of a vote, they felt guerrilla verbal tactics were justified in order to influence those who did have control. I would argue that the world, especially intellectuals, scholars, media policy wonks, and politicians have now adopted their methods.

Chapter 2.

Toying with the Truth

Traditionally in academia, at least since the Renaissance, the scientific method has become more and more the standard by which academics accept truth. "Suspected" facts, gathered and tested, provided the means by which to inform all rational decisions. As more facts were gathered and tested in more circumstances, the shape of the "truth" would gradually morph, of course, but that was built into the scientific method. It wasn't perfect, but it was the best that non-omniscient human beings could do, and despite many scientific clashes and feuds, it has served humankind well.

However, in subjects that were less fact-oriented, it is more difficult to determine "truths". Mathematical truths are less controversial than scientific truths, while scientific truths are less controversial than truths about human psychology or sociological behaviors. Historical occurrences were recorded but might not have been recorded objectively, and so their "truths" are debatable. Interpretations of literature are even more subject to debate. In literature, however, rather than debate about a universally accepted truth, academics simply accept that each of them could have their own interpretations. My interpretation of *Hamlet* may not be yours, but since we cannot know Shakespeare's intent, we simply recognize different interpretations until more details about the history of the play can be brought to light. In fact, we laud Shakespeare for writing a play so rich in meaning that it could sustain several interpretations.

In politics, one uses both political theory (which a branch of philosophy akin to sociological theory) and recorded history to advocate for a point of view. Often that point of view may have an economic element as well. The mathematical aspect of economics is seldom in question, however the intended mathematical *inputs* (e.g. potential tax revenues, proposed tax incentives, marketplace innovations, cultural preferences for spending, etc.) are not calculable in a scientific way. The human element throws a large and very important variable into economic assessments in particular, and political assessments in general. Thus, one goes to history to determine the likely result of a proposed political or economic/political action.

History, however, is subject to interpretation, as well. I recently saw an article that reprised certain historical events that occurred when I was a college student. The author, not alive at the time, engaged in what I considered to be a revisionist history and evaluation of those events. "What kind of authority can he have in making these claims?" I thought, "He was not even on the planet when they happened." It was reasonable, I thought, that my version of these events was more accurate than his. In reality, however, I learned about them second hand just as he had. *I had the advantage and disadvantage of immediacy.* He had the advantage and disadvantage of several other writers' years of reflection. So, in sum, it would be difficult to say which of our versions of this history was more accurate. However, there was another important factor in the search for accuracy in his article. I had the advantage of not having had a political bias at the time of the relevant events. He had the disadvantage of writing in today's world in which his political leanings are quite likely to influence his point of view. In fact, I believe that if he did not have a political point of view, his article would probably not have been published.

History is 5/7ths "story" and stories can be factual or fictional. All stories must go through a storyteller before they can be digested by a story-consumer. Thus, even supposed factual stories can be slanted by the unconscious presumptions and creative images or descriptions of the storyteller. A story writer sets a mood with carefully chosen words and carefully selected scenes. For example, "John then proceeded to walk the fifty feet to the drug store where he was shot and killed by one of the perpetrators of a robbery in progress" reads quite differently from the more creative and less objective, "Unaware that this was his last day on earth, John Smith, father of two, walked briskly down the street he had strolled so many times before, eager to buy his twin daughters the formula that his beautiful wife Janey preferred. He no doubt had a lift in his step and a smile on his face since he was proud to provide for his three ladies. He did not know that they would ever see him alive again."

The storyteller is the medium by which the event is transferred to others. Thus, several storytellers might be called "the media". Ask yourself if media reporting is factual, objective, and unbiased. Ask yourself how much of the media's coverage of contemporary history-in-the-making is fictional story.

Our interpretations of the story aspect of history are influenced not only by unconscious personal preferences, but also by our experiences with those who review movies, plays, and written fiction, even if they have no intention to slant the truth. Here I do not mean only professional reviewers, but also professors of literature and other teachers that, without intending bias, teach their students how to enrich their enjoyment of stories through intelligent interpretation. I am always fascinated when I hear yet another interpretation of a scene from *Hamlet*. After 400+ years, one would think that we have been sated with such interpretations, but this is not always the case. The good writing of an author who understands psychology and social interactions will sometimes yield deeper and deeper insights into what he/she could have meant. Teasing out these insights is a skill that *does not produce truths per se, but possibilities*. Similarly, teasing out insights from history results not in truths, but in possibilities. Applying the scientific method to history as far as possible, one should attempt to find corroborating evidence for an interpretation that would convince a story-consumer that those possibilities are likely to be factual.

Fiction writers can afford to be fanciful because the only tether to facts required is a context in which readers are willing to suspend their disbelief. Even fantasy fiction writers, as wild and experimental as they may wish to be, cannot not afford to create a situation where a magic wand that, in chapter one, makes a character float in the air inexplicably turns into a magic turnip that makes the character burp in chapter two. Unless the writer is aiming for absurd humor, the reader will simply not accept the variability of that context. *You have set my expectations,* the reader thinks, *now, stick to them.*

Even when interpreting a piece of literature, scholarly students as well as their teachers, are expected to given reasons for their conclusions. I was teaching English Literature at Cambridge School of Weston one summer when a friend and future roommate of mine who was a Math and Science teacher in the same program walked in while I was taking notes on one of Salinger's *Nine Stories* that I had planned to teach that week. Seeing me alternate between pensive and active states, he asked me what I was doing. I said that I was relating sections of a Salinger story each to the other in order to support an interpretation. He still did not seem to understand.

"Well, I have to rationally justify my point-of-view, don't I?" I said.

"What? *You do that?*"

"Of course," said I, "how else would I convince anyone that I might be correct? You do that in math and science, don't you?"

"Wow! Yes, but I thought that English Lit was just reading a story and then sitting around discussing how you *feel* about it." Obviously, his English Lit education had not been as academically rigorous as his education in the sciences had been.

Several decades ago, journalists began to be educated in universities rather than on the streets or in the newsrooms of city journals. Journalism graduates employed by newspapers wrote their news stories as if they were beginning the first chapter of a novel. They did not follow the old rules of revealing the Who, What, Where, When, Why, and How of the story as early as possible, but took the reader on a more leisurely and sometimes more pleasant journey in which those W's and H's would eventually be revealed. They wrote as if they were frustrated fiction writers, setting a mood, telling the tale indirectly and with color, thus making it *feel* more real, and thereby subtly slanting their coverage. Any attempt at objectivity was blithely ignored in favor of readability. That may have sold newspapers, but it did nothing to advance objective journalism—making an average person's access to the truth (or a close approximation thereof) more difficult.

In a similar development, the objectivity and accuracy of TV journalism took a hit when cable TV went 24/7 with its news broadcasts. In the pre-cable days, although the headlines often seemed repetitious, there was enough news to fill the noon, early evening, and nighttime slots. However, with a constant news cycle on cable TV, commentary, editorializing, and punditry were needed to fill the gaps. As a result, we do not get history-in-the-making, but his or her story in the making, with all the interpretation and political filtering that implies.

Finally, as if 24/7 TV news were not enough, we have Internet podcasts, available on demand, that on one hand can broaden the perspective of the viewer, but on the other hand require the viewer to have three heads and no hours of sleep in order to take in all the viewpoints.

Both to entertain the audience and to fill the need for content, we have an array of opinions, *the most outlandish of which garner the most attention.* Remember when Hollywood Stars were accused of pulling publicity stunts to get coverage in magazines and TV so that people would pay more attention to them, thus potentially boosting their box-office draw and their personal compensation when employed? The news version of the publicity stunt, the outlandish opinion, is essentially how we now get our information—the raw input from which we are to glean the "truth". And gleaning truth from hype is something we are ill equipped to do.

If we cannot readily discern the truth, how do we judge what we support, for whom we will vote, or in what we believe? We tend to support, vote for, and believe with limited information and a large dependence on our gut-feelings. So, if you wanted to influence someone to agree with you, what would you do? Would you make a rational argument with which most reasonable people, reporters, newscasters, or intellectuals would *have* to agree due to their dedication to the truth and the logic of the scientific method? Or, would you try to influence their gut feelings?

If you chose the emotional route, you can use two tactics, or a combination of both. You can get them to feel bad for you and guilty for how they made you feel or you can express your anger, making them fear either your retaliation or the loss of your affection. Sounds like guerrilla tactics to me.

Chapter 3.

Out of Context

Let's start by dealing with a few of those ways a "pre-feminist" might express her displeasure to an offending man in her life. By the way, I do not wish to imply that any specific point-of-view, if used in an example, is right or wrong, nor do I wish to imply that a pre-feminist woman would necessarily be wrong in being upset with a guy. None of this has to do with substance. It has to do with method. In offering examples in this book, I had first planned to relate actual events that happened to me or to those I have known, but by doing that, inevitably I would be accused of taking sides, misinterpreting what happened, or being a mean-spirited guy intending to embarrass the women in question.

See? That's what I mean. The very chance that I would have to deal with that accusation made me reconsider and invent semi-fictional situations (based on actual situations, of course) where no living being could be readily recognized and no personal offense could be easily assumed. To be honest, I am sorry to say that those who prefer to take offense will do so anyway, and those people will probably take it personally, as well—an example of "taking something out of context", and of "mind reading".

Of the following items, the items in **bold** will be illustrated in the succeeding story.

"PRE-FEMINIST" EMOTIONAL ARGUMENTATION TACTICS

- **Taking something out of context**
- **All accidents or coincidences will be interpreted as if they had been intended**
- **Misquoting/intentionally misinterpreting**
- Exaggerating the alleged problem
- Taking one aspect of what you say and completing the narrative with their own implications
- **Jumping to extreme conclusions/actions**
- **Mind reading**
- **Drawing conclusions based on facts that**

could have other interpretations

- **Assuming that the opposite party means something they may not mean**
- Looking for anything that justifies a biased narrative
- **Dwelling on what the other side doesn't do, rather than evaluating what it does**
- Attempting to "win" (or have the other party give in) rather than find the objective truth
- Never taking the blame for anything/never admitting she is wrong
- Assuming that "since I know I am virtuous, you cannot be".

VIGNETTE #1

Abigail and Andy just started dating and are now discussing how to improve his website. His online business sells specialty books and videos most of which are his own creations. He doesn't make a lot of money, but he needs the site to be attractive and function well for customers because the little he earns will soon become his main retirement income. Abigail has a lot of experience with an online business that she ran in another state years before, when she was married. She advises Andy about the user-friendliest way to set up his webpages and arrange his content, as well as make his site rank more highly with search engines. She then suggests hiring a service to maximize his site's presence on search engines. Having previously hired two separate web-design firms who not only delivered a poor product but also could not follow his directions, costing him money he could not afford to waste, he was not given to taking a chance on another firm. "Well," Abigail says, "you need to spend money to make money. But it's your site, so it's your choice."

Andy confirms a dinner date with Abigail for Saturday evening. "I'll call you when I'm leaving my house. I'll try to arrive early so I can avoid the traffic." All is well. He arrives at 5:30 PM and asks if she is ready to go out, but she says she's used to having dinner at 8:00 PM and invites him in. She serves several appetizers and they sit on her bed eating, talking, and watching TV. One thing leads to another and before they know it, they have made love twice and the time is now approaching 10:00 PM. "Too late for dinner now," Andy says, "but I'll take you out for breakfast, if that's okay. As I said, I have to leave at 1:00 PM since I have an appointment at 3:00 PM, but that should give us plenty of time for breakfast."

Abigail sleeps past 11:00 AM, and when she finally arrives in the kitchen, Andy has made coffee for her and asks if she'd like toast. They have a low-key breakfast and he asks her for a dinner-date at his place for the following Friday. "I hate to leave," he says, "but my appointment is important. Looking forward to next weekend. Can I do anything for you before I go?"

Abigail hugs him and says, "Let's make love one more time."

Two days later, he emails Abigail, writing, "Looking forward to Friday. Is there anything special you'd like me to have around the house? And are there any kinds of food you especially like, so I can plan the evening?"

The next day he receives a return email: "I believe you lied to me. You should have taken me out for dinner last Saturday and you didn't—just to save money. Instead, you pigged out on my cheese and crackers. I want nothing more to do with you."

COMMENTARY

Many guys would throw up their hands and simply say that Abigail was crazy. Women may see it differently—not that she was being absolutely fair, but that she recognized actions from Andy that appeared suspicious. His actions might also seem suspicious if they reminded her of similar events that occurred at another time with another person. Perhaps her former husband was a notorious skinflint. Perhaps he had lied to her or promised her things that he never delivered. Both men and women evaluating Abigail's response can see that she did not garner enough information to legitimately accuse Andy of similar actions, but perhaps because she had been so hurt by her husband's deeds, she became hyper-sensitive to anything that *felt* the same.

POLITICAL COUNTERPARTS

There is a TV show in which intellectuals of various viewpoints are invited to contrast and compare their reasoning.

Mr. Ares Jefferson believes that the government should, in the vast majority of cases, stay out of race relations. He argues that unless rights are being infringed, people of any race have the personal wherewithal to earn money and make a better-than-average living for themselves without the government's legal favoritism or monetary handouts.

Professor Antonio Jackson believes that government must give certain racial groups lower taxes, and interest-free loans to buy businesses in their neighborhoods. He argues that in ten years these business could start paying back the loans and in twenty-five years, the government help-program would no longer be necessary.

Moderator: Since neither of your points of view have been put into practice, there is no empirical evidence by which to evaluate which method would best serve the minority community, or the broader culture. How can we know how to proceed?

Prof. Jackson: Mr. Jefferson does not believe in investing government funds in order to help a segment of the population that desperately needs it. That seems shortsighted. Perhaps he should read my book, *Why Minorities Have The Right to Major Government Investments*.

Mr. Jefferson: Those government funds you speak of are derived from taxes, so it is the government's duty to use them efficiently and effectively. Your plan for curtailing tax revenue and lending money that might never be repaid sounds to me like a formula for another government boondoggle, or at least an endless pit, especially since previous government investments since The Great Society have not resulted in the successes they predicted.

Jackson: So you are both cheap and racially insensitive then.

Jefferson: No, I am fiscally responsible. Race has nothing to do with it. All races have the human capacity, if they experience no interference, to pull themselves up.

Jackson: Mr. Moderator, I would suggest that we have learned a lot since The Great Society and that not to attempt to help is, in essence, racist!

Sound familiar? In each case, both the male/female relationship and the political discussion, one party (Abigail in the former and Jackson in the latter) used at least some of the following kinds of tactics:

- **Taking something out of context**
- **Interpreting all accidents or coincidences as if they had been intended**
- **Misquoting/intentionally misinterpreting**
- **Jump to extreme conclusions/actions**
- **Mind reading**
- **Drawing conclusions based on facts that could have other interpretations**
- **Assuming that the opposite party means something they may not mean, and**
- **Dwelling on what other side *doesn't* do, rather than evaluating what it does.**

Did they do this intentionally or have they simply become used to arguing this way? In both cases, neither Abigail nor Jefferson try to understand the other side's context, but assume the worse of their "opponents", emphasizing what the other side allegedly would *not* do in the future, rather than investigating similar situations in the past to help decide what the future might bring under one plan or the other.

How captured were you by the content of what they said rather than the method by which they argued? Content is important, of course, but if the *method of argumentation* does not defend one's position, but is used to attack the opponent, you might wish to think twice about the value of the content it supports.

Chapter 4.

It Must Be Bias

Here's another little vignette. Have you experienced something like this before? And once again here is my list of "pre-feminist" or "guerrilla" tactics, the relevant ones in bold print.

- Taking something out of context
- Interpreting all accidents or coincidences as if they had been intended
- Misquoting/intentionally misinterpreting
- **Exaggerating the alleged problem**
- **Taking one aspect of what you say and completing the narrative with their own implications**
- Jumping to extreme conclusions/actions
- Mind reading

- **Drawing conclusions based on facts that could have other interpretations**
- Assuming that the opposite party means something they may not mean
- **Looking for anything that justifies a biased narrative**
- Dwelling on what other side *doesn't* do, rather than evaluating what it does
- Attempting to "win" (or have the other party give in) rather than find the objective truth
- Never taking the blame for anything/never admits she is wrong
- **Since I know I am virtuous, you cannot be.**

VIGNETTE #2

"You have done this before!" Betty calls into the phone.

"Done what?" Bob asks.

"You laughed at me."

"But Betty, I wasn't laughing at you! I was laughing at...."

"You laughed right into my face, Bob! You can't tell me you didn't just laugh."

Bob takes a breath to calm his irritation. "Yes, I did, but not at you. Let me explain."

"Don't you dare! You couldn't have meant anything else but an insult!"

"Betty! Have I ever insulted you? I was laughing at…."

"Don't explain! It will just make everything feel worse! You always have an excuse for everything!"

COMMENTARY

In the above vignette, wouldn't you like to know what actually happened between the two, and Bob's reason for laughing? In addition, wouldn't it be nice to know why Betty jumped to a conclusion, and was convinced she could not be wrong? Why did she assume that Bob was insulting her without listening to his explanation? Was she used to being insulted by other men or did she actually *want* to take offense?

If we state what actually happened, however, we would have to do so from an omniscient point of view, like the narrator of a story, but that would make you concentrate on the details of the event (the empirical data) rather than on the mode of argumentation.

Assume that Bob had truly done something insensitive. That would justify Betty's pique, but would it justify her method of argumentation? Alternately, assume that Bob actually did nothing wrong and that Betty misunderstood him. What does *that* say about her method of expressing her displeasure?

There are methods of expressing oneself that can describe how one personally feels without having to assume any negativity on the other person's part. When people use tactics as listed in bold above, it is likely that they have ulterior motives or that they simply want to win, rather than to sort out the truth or to preserve the relationship. When people simply want to win, they are using guerrilla maneuvers because they have already determined that, as the assumed enemy, you must be wrong.

POLITICAL COUNTERPARTS

"It is clear to me," the congresswoman explains to the host of the radio interview, "that the party in power does not want children to live a comfortable life. They have done this many times before, not voting for additional school breakfast benefits when it is clear that lunch alone is not enough."

The host suggests that there was more to this argument then what was being presented. "Congresswoman Burke, when your party was in power two years ago, you successfully voted in a school breakfast program."

"Yes, thank goodness. It is keeping children, whose parents do not feed them well, nourished enough to last a full day in school."

"The party now in power is not trying to revoke the program. Rather, it is simply refusing a 20% increase in funding."

"Why are you trying to make excuses for them? The kids *need* that additional funding!"

Sound familiar? In each case, both the woman in the relationship (Betty) and the member of congress in the political discussion (Congresswoman Burke) used at least some of the following tactics:

- **Exaggerate the alleged problem**
- **Taking one aspect of what you say and completing the narrative with their own implications**
- **Drawing conclusions based on facts that could have other interpretations**
- **Looking for anything that justifies a biased narrative**
- **Since I know I am virtuous, you cannot be.**

Did they do this consciously or have they simply become used to arguing this way? Neither Betty nor Burke explains why they are so emotional about the issue. No facts are given, so there is nothing specific to discuss. Instead, the *emotionality* of the claim is meant to convince either Bob in one case, or the radio audience in the other, of the validity of whatever they say.

SPECIFICS TO GENERALIZATIONS

Beware of the emotional argument that promotes an incident or even several incidents as a general truth. For example: A cop shoots an unarmed man. A court rules it an unlawful shooting and he is disciplined with a 60-day suspension. Instead of arguing that the police officer should have received a sterner sentence, the emotional argument is that since one unarmed man was shot, and since he was black, the police must be hunting all black men on a daily basis. The initial item is a verifiable fact. The generalization drawn from that item cannot be verified either by statistics or personal experiences. In fact, it is **an exaggeration of the alleged problem**.

Generalizations can be completely legitimate—without them it is difficult to talk about large groups or overarching concepts. Generalization suggests that once one knows a number of facts about X, one can predict something about X to a high percentage of accuracy. In other words, a generalization based on facts gives one an edge in estimating a probable outcome. Is that outcome always correctly estimated? Of course, not, but it is estimated correctly a large percentage of the time, so the generalization is therefore legitimate. For example, to say that Swedish women tend to be taller than Indonesian women can be proven by statistics, even though you can always find a specific Indonesian woman who is taller than a specific Swedish woman.

Generalization is necessary; stereotyping is not. Stereotyping is akin to both mysticism and racism in that it is a bias that claims personality characteristics must be true by dint of an immutable quality, physical, locational, historical, or otherwise. I remember Italian aunts who used to warn me against people born on Christmas Eve. Why? Because they had the "evil eye". "But, Great Aunt Ophelia, what does that mean?" If any "evidence" were given, it would always be a specific example, like: "My cousin's friend had the evil eye and two of her husbands passed away before they were 60!" To Great Aunt Ophelia, that was sufficient evidence to believe in "the evil eye", even though many men pass away before they are 60, even when they are married to women not born on December 24th.

Whenever a debate opponent uses a single example to represent a larger generality, he/she is drawing a conclusion for you. Take care to search for validating statistics as well as more than a few specific examples.

CONCRETES TO PRINCIPLES TO CONCRETES

Specifics forced into generalizations should not be confused with an overwhelming number of cases from which you can draw a hypothesis (a generalization) that can be tested. Testing the hypothesis allows one to formulate principles. Principles can, in turn, predict concrete examples. A cop shoots an unarmed man. A court rules it an unlawful shooting and he is suspended for 60 days. After having researched similar shootings over the last 20 years, you can argue authoritatively that the policeman's union has constrained police departments to discipline the officer rather than to fire him. Your concrete fact is the actual shooting. Your principle is that police unions protect unlawfully acting police officers so they never leave the force. Your concrete prediction is that a similar shooting will happen again somewhere in the country, probably within a year, with a similar result.

Chapter 5.

Mind Reading

Here's a third set of vignettes. Many of these tactics either assume that the tacticians can read the mind of their opposite number, or that they want a third party to believe that they have inside information. Again, the tactics used in the examples are in **bold** below.

- Taking something out of context
- Interpreting all accidents or coincidences as if they had been intended
- Misquoting/intentionally misinterpreting
- Exaggerating the alleged problem

- **Taking one aspect of what you say and completing the narrative with their own implications**
- **Jumping to extreme conclusions/actions**
- **Mind reading**
- **Drawing conclusions based on facts that could have other interpretations**
- **Assuming that the opposite party means something they may not mean**
- Looking for anything that justifies a biased narrative
- Dwelling on what other side *doesn't* do, rather than evaluating what it does
- Attempting to "win" (or have the other party give in) rather than find the objective truth
- Never taking the blame for anything/never admits she is wrong
- Since I know I am virtuous, you cannot be.

VIGNETTE #3

"Have you noticed this article?" Professor Charles asked one of his graduate students. Whom do you think Professor Churuzo is talking about here?"

After only a minute of reading, the student said, "That's got to be you, sir."

"I think so. Keep reading, if you will."

"She says you used her private teaching method without permission. But Professor, I was there when both of you introduced the details of her method in a public seminar. She was partnering with you. I've got a video of it. And you always were careful to give her credit."

"Yes, and yet here she says that in my new book I merely changed some details and that I'm passing off her methods as my own." Professor Charles was half annoyed, half incredulous.

"But your book gives her credit and simply extends the teaching in your own way. Isn't that what scholarship is about—learning from other sources, giving them credit, and then extending the knowledge with further study?"

"Of course," said Professor Charles. "There must have been some misunderstanding along the way. I'll call her and tell you what happened next time I see you."

One week later…

"Sir, did you call Professor Churuzo?"

"I did. She did not answer, so I left a message. I told her that I have always respected her and that I would not, and did not, plagiarize or use her material without credit."

"And?"

"And she did not call back."

COMMENTARY

Has someone disappointed you to the extent that you are willing to cut ties with that person? It has happened to me a couple of times, from both directions—someone thinking ill of me enough to cut ties and my thinking ill of them enough to cut ties. And, of course, the closer I felt to them, the more it hurt. It seems that the best a person can do when confronted with such disappointment is to have a conversation with the opposite party to make sure there is no misunderstanding. Unfortunately, the passive aggressive nature of some guerrilla warfare and pre-feminist tactics means that that conversation may never happen. Since they feel they understand you well enough to know what you think and why you think it, they feel perfectly justified in drawing their conclusions and acting in a way that is more extreme than they might have acted if a conversation with you had occurred. Worse still is that their passive aggressive response makes them feel justified in publicizing their opinions as if they were facts in an attempt to garner sympathy or gather advocates while simultaneously attempting to "justifiably" and publicly besmirch your character.

POLITICAL COUNTERPARTS

Consider any presidential elections that have occurred during your lifetime. Look at the claims one party had made about the other party's candidate. Then consider how likely it may have been that the claim was at least an exaggeration and perhaps an outright lie. This is not to say that all presidential candidates are flawless, but that exaggerations of past flaws in an attempt to describe their current characters can be unfair, and that extreme exaggerations or lies about their character are dishonest. The worst part of this kind of tactic is that it obfuscates objective truth so that people do not know what to believe and thus they run to their "tribal leaders" hoping that the leaders, in their superior knowledge, will decide the truth for them.

Here are some (not all) examples of political claims that have been made in presidential elections since 1960 and the likely truth that was obfuscated in the heat of the race. Note how many these claims depended on "mind reading" (see **bold** in CLAIM column).

Committed partisans may argue with aspects of this chart. No matter what the truth actually was, *there was an actual truth*. However, regardless of the objective truth, one side exaggerated a perceived negative about the opposite side, in order to win favor with the voting public. Often the method used is one side's *coming to a conclusion* for the public that would have required *reading the other side's mind*.

YEAR	CANDIDATE (election winner in **bold**)	CLAIM ("mind reading" example in **bold**)	LIKELY TRUTH (If Any)
1960	**Kennedy (D)** vs. Nixon	**Kennedy, being Catholic, would in effect cede control of the country to The Vatican.**	An unwarranted fear portrayed as if it were likely.
1964	**Johnson (D)** vs. Goldwater (R)	**If elected, Goldwater would use nuclear bombs in Vietnam.**	In an interview, Senator Goldwater had said only that all options for fighting the Vietnam War should be on the table.
1968	**Nixon (R)** vs. Humphrey (D) vs. Wallace (CAI)		
1972	**Nixon (R)** vs. McGovern (D)		
1976	Ford (R) vs. **Carter (D)**		
1980	Carter (D) vs. **Reagan (R)** vs. Anderson (I)	Reagan was a cowboy, not a serious politician, and **a warmonger** (calling him "Ronald Ray Gun").	An unwarranted claim based on his film career before becoming governor of CA.
1984	**Reagan (R)** vs. Mondale (D)	**Reagan was too old to be competent.**	Reagan was the oldest elected president; however, competence was not an issue during his first term.

1988	**G. H. W. Bush (R)** vs. Dukakis (D)	**Bush was a wimp.**	An unwarranted claim based on his wearing glasses, while ignoring his WWII piloting.
1992	G. H. W. Bush (R) vs. **W. Clinton (D)** vs. Perot (I)	**Bush camp claimed that Perot was a Clinton-campaign plant meant to draw away his votes.**	Although Perot did draw from Bush's total, there is no evidence that his campaign was set up by Clinton.
1996	**Clinton (D)** vs. Dole (R) vs. Perot (I) vs. Nader (G)	Democrats were accused of accepting money from Chinese government.	While there was a lot of circumstantial evidence that this occurred, there never was a smoking gun.
2000	Gore (D) vs. **G. Bush (R)** vs. Nader (G)	Bush was a drunk and draft dodger.	Bush once pleaded guilty to a DUI charge before entering politics. He did receive favorable treatment to enlist in the Air National Guard, but did not dodge the draft.
2004	**Bush (R)** vs. Kerry (D)		
2008	**Obama (D)** vs. McCain (R)	Obama was not born in the USA.	According to a duplicated birth certificate, he was born in Hawaii.
2012	**Obama (D)** vs. Romney (R)	Romney had not paid his taxes.	A lie. Romney had paid all his taxes.
2016	H. Clinton vs. **Trump (R)**	Many claims on both sides.	Too soon at this writing to objectively sort out the truth.

Chapter 6.

Digital Thinking

- Taking something out of context
- Interpreting all accidents or coincidences as if they had been intended
- Misquoting/intentionally misinterpreting
- Exaggerating the alleged problem
- Taking one aspect of what you say and completing the narrative with their own implications
- Jumping to extreme conclusions/actions
- Mind reading
- Drawing conclusions based on facts that could have other interpretations

- Assuming that the opposite party means something they may not mean
- Looking for anything that justifies a biased narrative
- Dwelling on what other side *doesn't* do, rather than evaluating what it does
- **Attempting to "win" (or have the other party give in) rather than find the objective truth**
- **Never taking the blame for anything/never admits she is wrong**
- **Since I know I am virtuous, you cannot be.**

The last item on the list above is an underlying implication in much of the argumentation that occurs in today's political "discussions". I have mentioned previously that once you think of your opposite number as your enemy, you cannot allow him/her any benefit of the doubt. But since you are not really at war, a war footing is blatantly inappropriate and, in fact, is not a good strategy for unifying sides, or in some cases, even for winning a war.

A former girlfriend of mine had a boss who used to regularly reference "the tyranny of the OR"—the idea that in a discussion there can be only two sides. Greg Gutfeld (on TV's *The Five*) frequently bemoans the use of this same digital thinking, calling it "the prison of two ideas".

Eldridge Cleaver in his iconic Soul on Ice, referring to the then current Civil Rights struggle stated, "If you are not part of the solution, you are part of the problem." Although he was successful in making his point, I think his statement was an oversimplification. Let's say Duke Dangerfield was an unapologetic racist. His parents and the area in which he grew up have conditioned his mind to believe that one race is clearly inferior to another. Over the years, his teachers and his minister have gently tried to convince him that his ideas on race are inaccurate, but he is obstinate. He has never taken any action that would curtail actual civil rights for members of another race, never harassed them, or persecuted them, however his beliefs have not changed. If he does not change his beliefs to support equal civil rights for everyone, he is certainly not part of "the solution"; however, as long as he does not interfere with the application of equal civil rights for everyone, neither is he part of "the problem". Despite his unpopular viewpoint, as a free person, he can think whatever he wants. Most of us may disagree with his bias and some may even avoid interacting with him. But his freedom is not subject to the digital choice Eldridge Cleaver, and others since that time, have set up.

Currently in American society, there are many who argue that it's "either my way or the highway" or "Silence =

Compliance" or "non-racist must be replaced with anti-racist". In essence, these statements attempt to shame people into joining a cause and accepting an extreme without deliberation and without exception. They are saying, "If you do not agree with me and join my cause, you must be absolutely wrong and may even be immoral since you are 'part of the problem'."

MANICHAEAN CHOICES

The Persian prophet Mani founded a religion in the third century AD in which the entire universe was divided into good vs. evil, light vs. dark, left vs. right, etc. A Manichean choice then is a digital choice. Either you switch the light on or keep it off. "Ah," you say, having read my above denial of digital thinking, "but you can install a dimmer switch." True, but even if the light were dim, it is still ON rather than OFF. Manichaean choices do, in fact, exist.

A Manichaean would say, "Either you are in the car or you are outside the car."

"Ah, but you can sit in the car with the door open and one foot out."

"True, but can you find the middle ground between the car running or not running?"

"Well, at the moment it is being started, is the brief time of running and not running."

"That is pretty fine hair-splitting," the Manichaean argues. "The car can be moving or not moving. Either you drove over the speed limit or under the speed limit. Either you hit another object or you did not. In the same way, either you are a member of the gang or you are not."

"Well," you contend, "I could be a non-practicing member, like a non-church going Catholic or a non-holiday-observant Jew."

"But still you would have described yourself as Catholic or Jew. Now, what if the rules say that you must commit at least one felony a year to remain in good standing with the gang? It would be difficult for you to be a wishy-washy member."

Every election day in the U.S., you face a digital choice. While it is true that sometimes a third or fourth party arises, for practical purposes, at least at this writing, either a Democrat or a Republican will be elected. "But I can choose not to vote at all!" you argue. True, that would break your personal digital choice, but it would not change the collective digital choice. For example, I once explained my personal de facto digital outcome to some strangers talking politics in a pub. "We live in Massachusetts," I said. "Democrats outnumber Republicans three-to-one. When voting for president, I am all but disenfranchised. If I vote Democrat, my vote does not count since it will be a blue drop lost in the blue wash. If I vote Republican, my vote does not count since the blue wash will drown my red drop. And if I vote for a third party or do not vote at all, my vote will not count because the color of the wash has been preset." Apparently, I face a Manichaean choice that seems to be no choice at all

And yet, Massachusetts often elects Republican governors. How does that happen? It happens because there is a very large group of independents that can tint the water one color or the other. I am not ignoring the idea that one can be faced with a true Manichaean choice, rather I resist the idea that all emotional choices have to be Manichaean.

One summer, when I was but a youth, my father was escorting my mother and I through Kenmore Square in Boston after having attended a Red Sox game in Fenway Park just down the street. A group of men burst out of a bar and one of them was assaulting a waiter. None of the spectators did anything about it. I expected my father to break it up, but he scurried my mom and I away from the hassle and toward our parked car. Rather than taking sides, he took a third way. In this case, it was the responsible way. But one could also argue that one of the spectators or one of the bar's employees had a Manichaean choice—to help or to stay passive. When people advocate "silence = compliance" this is the type of situation they are envisioning. I use this example to illustrate that there may come a time when one feels obliged to act because of one's principles, despite the risk; however, I would question whether an heroic bar employee could realistically expect to cajole other spectators into action. If he defended the waiter, kudos to him, but he would have no right, for example, to shame my father into abandoning his family in order to join the fight, as if he had only a Manichaean choice.

How many people, who believe that "climate change" is an impending crisis, will call those who disagree with them "science deniers"? Even those that disagree may respect science, but may simply read the facts differently. Why does one side feel obliged to shame or insult the other side into submission? Could part of the climate change argument be correct and another part wrong? Why does it have to be either/or? Since when is our thinking about an issue required to be digital?

I'd like to offer two answers that are likely to annoy both sides of a digital debate.

AFRAID TO BE SOLO

It's not exactly a news flash that people enjoy the company of other people. In fact, people especially like people who are like them. That's why people gather under various common "causes" like clubs, teams, political parties, charities, etc. Gathering together allows a person to feel that he or she is not the only one who knits, plays hacky sack, supports The Green Socialists of Wall Street, or gives to The Veteran's Society for Plumpness in Dogs. Social interaction helps accomplish goals and helps create friendships. Very few people like to feel alone. There is a reason the punishment for crimes is isolation from society in prison, and that punishment in prison is solitary confinement.

Social people often encourage friends to be social in the same social circles in which they are social. So shall it be with social movements that have political propensities. The larger the movement, the more influence it is likely to have. However, many political assemblages also spawn opposition so that opponents will produce their own political assemblages. And so the competition begins. Which groups will be larger? Which group will be more influential?

If you cannot persuade people to pursue your political platform via lucid logic, you might do so with passionate parlance. If passionate parlance poops out, you can always claim that not being on your side is immoral and morality requires a choice—a Manichaean choice—either you are with us or you are part of the problem.

RELIGION, SITUATION ETHICS, AND THE MORAL HIGH GROUND

For almost two thousand years, Christianity was the religion that dominated Western cultures. In order not to recognize any specific sect of Christianity, we refer to the general cultural dominance as the Judeo-Christian Tradition. Of course, since there is no single, unified Christianity, recognizing any specific sect would be unfair. The Catholic Church is divided into Roman Catholic and Eastern Orthodox which itself is divided into Russian, Armenian, and Greek Orthodox. Protestant churches not only have dozens of sects, but in some areas of the country each church can be a sect unto itself. One estimate holds that there are 33,000 Protestant sects. With such a lack of unity, it understandable that people summarize a set of teachings and beliefs as a generic Judeo-Christian Tradition, while they simultaneously recognize that any attempt at generalization will likely produce an exception.

Having noted this diversity, let us also note that, prior to the 1960s, a generic Judeo-Christian tradition was taken for granted as creating shared guidelines for moral behavior and values in the USA. The school day began with the Lord's Prayer. TV schedules either began or ended with a blessing. Politicians were not shy about saying, "God bless

America". Public and private ceremonies often began with an invocation from a guest minister, priest, or rabbi. Kids attended some version of Sunday school, whether or not it was on a Sunday, and families generally went to a house of worship during some part of the weekend.

The Judeo-Christian ethic, dominated by The Ten Commandments, provided a moral compass separate from official laws—the tradition provided a cultural impetus for people to conform to a generally accepted set of ethical guidelines without depending upon additional legal niceties.

Because of the Judeo-Christian tradition, the vast majority of citizens agreed on what was right versus what was wrong. However, those who may not have conformed to the preferred set of ethical behaviors felt that their freedoms, although not necessarily outlawed, were being culturally choked off. If you were atheist, gay, a follower of an unusual philosophy, or if you diverged from tradition in other ways, you felt you did not belong in the culture. In some cases, you were made to feel that you did not belong.

People that were comfortable with Judeo-Christian traditions and ethics believed that *they had the moral high ground*. They did not think it was in their purview to aggressively penalize non-conformers, but they certainly felt *they could ostracize them as much as legally possible*, and in extreme cases, make laws that opposed unconventional behaviors, even knowing that those laws were unlikely to be enforced (laws, for example, that prohibited cohabitation).

In the 1960s, the Baby Boomers, now entering college, challenged and even shrugged off many of the conventional ways of behaving. As those behaviors fell to the cultural wayside, the underlying values of Judeo-Christian ethics had fewer and fewer ways to manifest themselves. Those ethics were still in the culture, but saw the sun less often.

The '60s Generation perceived their society as one that had been historically successful in war, in post-war economic growth, and in scientific advancement, but "uptight" in cultural advancement. Their parents, the WWII "Greatest Generation" had lived through a depression and a world war capped by a war in Korea and was now grateful for a predictable, relatively risk-free life. It had won its freedom and now wanted to enjoy it. Its children, however, saw inconsistencies in the dominant traditional ethics and so they challenged their parents' generation's resistance to change. The risks that the WWII Generation took were physical. The risks that the Baby Boomers wanted to take were largely cultural.

With the new birth control pill, pregnancy (the biggest physical risk of premarital sex) was all but eliminated, so why not indulge? Instead of being stuck with one partner for fifty years, you could have several. Instead of marrying, you could live together.

Instead of sticking your neck out physically by fighting a war that the government (run by old WWII guys) wanted you to fight, you could stick your neck out morally, risking possible jail time, by avoiding the draft. In fact, the whole necessity for the draft was based on the idea of war. If you could stamp out war, you would not need a draft, and all people would be happier. That is, unless they were treated as second-class citizens.

It was obvious that since slavery had been abolished a century before, it was high time to abolish anything that re-sembled racism. The biggest physical risk that the Boomers took was in Freedom Riding and marching or demonstrat-ing in Jim Crow states. The Civil Rights Movement set the pattern for other cultural challenges that came on its heels: gay-rights and the second wave of feminism.

Ironically, even though the '60s Generation believed they were rebelling against the conventional practices of their parents by challenging the ethics and the sensibili-ties that their parents tried to teach them, those ethics and sensibilities had already been inculcated. In fact, although the manifestation of Judeo-Christian values had morphed, the values themselves were still the dominant lens through which the Boomers saw the world. Even though strict Judeo-Christian ethics were weakened by more fluid "situation ethics", the Boomers still felt that they were taking *the moral high ground.*

Without debating any of these cultural positions, please note that each generation, in turn, felt that they were *morally* correct. Prior to the 1960s, the WWII generation had the status and control to wag a collective finger at those young Americans who did not wish to conform. The Greatest Generation saw in nonconformity a potential risk to the status quo, a status quo that may not have been perfect, but was infinitely better than a depression, a world war, or living under a collectivist regime. In the 1960s, however, the children of the WWII Generation were becoming adults and would soon have cultural control. They saw a risk in maintaining any status quo that did not have as underpinning supports the ideals of peace, equality, and freedom for all.

Ironically, each generation from their moral high-perch was saying, "My way, or the highway. If you are not part of the solution, you are part of the problem. Make a digital decision!"

Frequently, along with the tyranny of the OR, comes hostility, because if you don't agree with me, you must be wrong. If I am on the moral high ground, you must be on the moral low ground; therefore, you must be immoral or even evil. It is easy, then, to start making one's arguments using these tactics and attitudes:

- **Attempting to "win" (or have the other party give in) rather than find the objective truth**
- **Never taking the blame for anything/never admits she is wrong**
- **Since I know I am virtuous, you cannot be.**

How do we avoid this digital thinking and the descent into enmity? How do we have a more cooperative society that is free, does not exclude people, but also does not allow its fundamental values to be endangered?

Perhaps investigating happier personal relationships will suggest answers.

Chapter 7.

A Happier Relationship

One of the disruptions either caused by, or made observable by, second wave feminism is the nature and quality of male-female relationships. If the woman feels she is not treated the way she wishes to be treated, she understandably advocates for herself, blaming her male counterpart for treating her that way. In my fictitious division of pre-1960 feminine attitudes and post-1960 feminist attitudes, I intentionally put the verbally facile, emotionally manipulative tactics of opposition on the side of the pre-feminists, as if a 1960 New Year's celebration could abruptly turn off tactics that had been used for generations, or as if women that now considered themselves feminists would suddenly forego such learned tactics. In reality, of course, this is not the case. Some traditional women did not become feminists. Others resisted the either/or choice and maintained their traditional roles while still advocating for equal pay, paid leave for child bearing, women's shelters, etc. Many women who embraced feminism as a *cause célèbre* still used the "pre-feminist" list of tactics. Advocates of other causes, I would argue, learned from them. A few feminist women were advocates for men as well as women, and boys as well as girls, and largely avoided our list of emotional tactics in their argumentation.

Gloria Steinem, famous for saying, "A woman needs a man like a fish needs a bicycle," also admitted, at a later date, that one mistake made in the women's movement was thinking that to be equal *to* a man, one had to be more *like* a man. This was an important point since equal rights cannot possibly mean identical behavior, identical attitudes, or identical preferences. If women could not be equal without becoming more like men, then why bother having a "Women's" Movement at all? Why not simply support a Transgender Movement, instead?

As the women's movement was gaining momentum, there were calls for more women to enter government and claims that women would make better national leaders than men because of their less belligerent natures, i.e. that *traits traditionally associated with women would be superior* to those traditionally associated with men. It would not be long before feminists would change that emphasis and assume that characteristics considered traditionally male were to be *imitated* even though feminists had previously opposed many of those characteristics in men. In neither case were feminists eager to enumerate the traditionally female characteristics that were preferable. For example, in an early interview, Steinem denied that women were better nurturers than men. What other characteristics, traditionally seen as female, would feminists deny in their quest for social equality? The more they shrugged off characteristics traditionally considered female in hopes of avoiding the implication that "female" meant "inferior", the more they backed themselves into the men's room.

If characteristics traditionally considered female are not worthy of respect equal to characteristics traditionally considered male, the idea of gender *differences* can no longer add important, albeit sometimes contradictory, sometimes complementary, elements to human cultures. If gender differences are not valuable, then feminists are receding into a digital choice—either act like traditionally unequal woman or act like a traditional man.

When women began to rise in positions of leadership previously held almost exclusively by men, they had to adopt the characteristic of competitiveness that men had developed through centuries of dominating sports, business, and politics. That competitiveness was probably in male DNA to begin with, but if it had originated socially (i.e. from nurture rather than from nature), it must have started at least as early as the hunter-gatherer days. During that era, the larger, stronger men would be the designated hunters, a job that required not only powerful spear arms, but also quiet teamwork and a strong desire to be victorious over the quarry. Those competitive achievements were used to advertise desirable masculine characteristics that would be selected by women who wanted their male children to inherit them. Stronger, more aggressive men secured the tribe's survival, and the tribe's survival, in turn, ensured the survival of those characteristics.

The supportive, nurturing attitudes attributed to women might also have had their origins in DNA, but if they had originated socially, they could easily have come from both childcare and from the communal groups that made gathering in the fields and forests more pleasant and safer. The interpersonal interactions of women also increased the chances of tribal and human survival by encouraging coop-eration with others, especially during birth and child rearing, the success of which made the tribe continue to exist. Interpersonal interactions also aided efficient gathering, the products of which afforded as much nourishment as the protein provided by the males. The characteristics that enhanced child rearing and efficient systems of gathering helped the tribe survive, and the tribe's survival ensured the survival of those characteristics.

In other words, males needed females and females needed males not just to reproduce but also to contribute to the survival of the tribe, and thus the survival of humankind. That interdependence functions best when male-female relationships function best.

Steinem may have been right that, in the post-1960s world, a woman needed a man like a fish needed a bicycle, but despite that presumption, bikes certainly still wanted to go fishing and fish certainly wanted to ride bikes. If men were completely useless to women, or vice versa, there would be no such thing as romantic relationships and thus no way to insure the survival of the "tribe".

RELATIONSHIP COMMUNICATION

How many times have you heard that the key to a successful romantic relationship is communication? Well, that depends on what you mean by communication. The "com" of communication means "with". "To commune" is to relate spiritually with someone. "Common", of course, means, "shared".

First, you have the act of talking to a person, but that could simply be complaining at rather than talking with a person. Then you have the act of listening, but that could be politely acting as an obtuse sounding board while not hearing what the other person has to say. To produce true communication, there must be a successful transfer of feelings or ideas from one person to another.

Does that successful transfer of information produce a more harmonious relationship? Not necessarily. What if Party A gets her message across clearly but Party B thinks the message is hogwash? Communication is achieved, but the relationship does not benefit. What if Party A explains herself but in a way that is offensive? Communication is achieved, but it may worsen the relationship.

In order for a relationship to be held together or improved, Party A must transmit her information successfully and Party B must be willing to receive and be willing to understand the information *from Party A's point of view*. But that's only half the story. Now, Party B must transmit successfully while Party A is willing to receive and understand the information *from Party B's point of view*. They may not end up agreeing, but they are more likely to end up understanding each other more fully. As important as transmitting and receiving in good faith is that both parties then respect their counterpart for having listened sincerely and having tried to understand their point of view.

This type of communication is exactly what is missing between those who hold allegedly opposing political points of view in the contemporary world. Full communication takes longer than people want to take, and takes more effort than people want to expend. In addition, any degrading of the effort to communicate or any subtle deceit will damage a recipient's inclination to listen and understand.

A political relationship can survive a certain level of gamesmanship as long as there is underlying mutual respect and both sides recognize that the gamesmanship is bound by rules. Once the acceptable limits of political gamesmanship are skirted, once deceit replaces attempts at understanding, the opponent's respect disappears, and one party recognizes that the other is trying to win no matter the cost. In national politics, for example, instead of both parties holding the shared value of the country's best interest or The Constitution's predominance, winning-at-any-cost means that one party holds itself as more valuable than the other party, The Constitution, or the country. This is when the final attitude on our tactics list emerges, first from the offending party and then, as a reaction, from the offended party: **Since I know I am virtuous, you cannot be.** In this way, enemies are created.

I ended the previous chapter by asking, "How do we avoid this digital thinking and the descent into enmity? How do we have a more cooperative society that is free, does not unjustifiably exclude, but also does not allow its fundamental values to be endangered?" To be frank, I do not believe that we can design a system that perfectly meets all these criteria; however, I do believe we can design a system that comes close. I hope to write a book, tentatively titled *The Flaws of Freedom* in which I explain that we constantly juggle the idea of total freedom with the idea of total inclusion, the idea of individual liberty with the idea of justice for all. However, one value has to dominate, I believe. We don't have to accept digital thinking, but we have to allow for thinking that is weighted one way or the other. In a relationship, this is called "compromise".

By no means do I want to advocate reactionary compromise. Those who think that compromise solves a problem find themselves the only one that compromise and the problem worsens. Rather, compromising by finding a proportional distribution of characteristics that harmonize well together is entirely another matter. Let's say that I like to talk 60% of the time, but so does my girlfriend. One or both of us will be frustrated at every conversation. However, if we recognize that we are hogging the decibels, we can voluntarily cede some air-time, gradually approaching a 50-50 compromise.

Many years ago, a French friend and I were driving from Paris to Chartres. We were discussing, as best I could in my broken French, a very similar idea. "Liberty, Fraternity, Equality" is the motto of France. They are wonderful ideals to which most countries would aspire; however, I said that, if taken literally, it is impossible to have all three in equal proportion. Liberty and Fraternity bond well together as do Fraternity and Equality, but Liberty and Equality have a more contentious relationship. If one is free, one is also free to be unequal. If one must be equal to his brother or sister, he is therefore not free. The only way Equality can bond with Liberty is to define Equality as equal rights under the law. The French nation did not want to choose one or the other, nor even two and not three. In different situations, different proportions of the mix are appropriate. And yet, getting the proportion correct for the situation at hand is quite a challenge. This is why digital thinking is so popular. Once a decision is made, there is no need to get the proportion right.

MIXING METHODS

You cannot compel a romantic partner or a political opponent to reject the use of emotional argumentative tactics. You can, of course, leave your romantic partner, but that's not so easy with political opponents. If you feel they are not playing fairly and you fight fire with fire, emotional tactic for emotional tactic, that choice tends to increase digital thinking rather than to eschew it, leaving people to choose between the more passionate emotional state. If you fight fire with inaction, your audience is liable to respond to your opponent's emotional appeal, thus you are unlikely to discourage your opponent from using apparently successful, if irrational, tactics.

What if you fight fire with water? In this case "water" is your making obvious to the audience the tactics the opponent is using. If you yourself were the audience to which the tactical appeal is directed, "water" is your being diligent in recognizing the use of these fiery emotional tactics, and perhaps also understanding the emotions elicited by the inverse point of view—fighting fire with fire while still holding the water hose. (More about fighting fire, not by firing back, but by setting back fires, in Chapter 11, *Dealing with Petulance.*)

In a free society, one convinces others via persuasion since threats and violence are prohibited. As a result, in any free society, a person will try to slant his presentation to maximize his ability to persuade. We see this every day in advertising. Advertisers are not legally allowed to lie, but they are allowed to overemphasize their positive selling points and obfuscate their negatives. Similarly, in creating an employment résumé, one emphasizes one's abilities and fails to mention one's drawbacks. In going out on a date, one shaves, showers, and shampoos when, on most Saturday nights, one would normally sit around in a t-shirt and sweatpants. It almost seems that persuasion gives people the license to lie—or almost lie.

That which balances the tendency to show only one's strong points, thus preventing that practice from being a lie, is that you know that the product has some less-than-desirable qualities, the applicant has some unstated drawbacks, and the person meeting you for a date doesn't sparkle quite so brightly during his/her leisure time.

"But," you may argue, "the average person who listens to a political argument already has a disposition to believe one side and not the other. How can I show those people that the party they tend to believe is playing fast and loose with the facts?"

There is a short-term and a long-term component to the answer. In the short-term, the most important thing is to state the truth and present empirical data to back up your claim. You might also offer the opposition some indulgence by recognizing aloud how difficult it is to sort out the objective truth and how easily a small error can lead one astray: "You know, I used to be of the same opinion. It seems reasonable, but when I studied the empirical data, I had to admit that as much as I wanted my former opinion to be true, I had to accept that it was not. Perhaps over time, with an objective review of the data, you may come to that conclusion independent of what I may think."

In the long-term, consider reading my little treatise called *10 Guideline Principles: Finding One's Way in a Messy World*, and try to live by those or similar guidelines. I hope adopting similar guidelines will help you directly, but your following them may also help you indirectly by gradually eliciting respect from others who value fairness and balance.

Spanning the short- and long-term, you can try to identify common values that occasionally will make an opponent more willing to agree with at least part of what you say, and will make your audience realize your good intent and your fairness. Toward that end, consider reading *10 Common Values to Unify a Contentious Culture.*

Vince Lombardi famously said, "Winning isn't everything. It's the only thing." As I asked in *10 Guideline Principles*, did Lombardi mean, since winning is the only thing, that he would be willing to cheat? I doubt it, and yet modern political strategists can use his quote as an American justification for domestic guerrilla warfare.

If winning is the only thing, ask yourself if Americans (or any national citizenry) would tolerate competing countries drugging their athletes to gain an advantage during the Olympics? Do we tolerate baseball players on steroids setting home run records? Do we ignore football teams stealing each other's playbooks? No, winning is NOT the only thing. To believe that it is starts a slide toward deceit and cheating. In politics, if the Republocrats or the Demagogocans feel that their winning is more important than the truth, more important than the welfare of the country, or more important than The Constitution, then their successfully winning elections through nefarious methods means that the party in power will be nefarious. If they cheat to get there, they will likely cheat while they hold office. If they lie to get elected, they will likely lie to the people who elected them.

As with many discussions on cultural and political challenges, the key variable is the *personal character* of the individuals that make up the parties, the voters, and the government. Ah, you may think, the author is advocating an old fashioned return to religion. Well, fine if that floats your boat, but I am actually advocating a return to personal accountability and ethical behavior, religious or otherwise.

Prior to the 1960s, the Judeo-Christian tradition (regardless of which specific religious sect drew one's adherence) presented us with a moral framework. But if that does not work for you today, there are other ways to go about acting morally. In *Your Ethics Are Immoral*, I discuss three major sources of ethical behavior, The Ethics of Divinity, The Ethics of Community, and The Ethics of Autonomy (with credit to Jonathan Haidt's book *The Righteous Mind*), and I try to help the reader evaluate each.

I mention my earlier social commentary books because I believe they link together with this volume to help the honest non-partisan see through the slanted partisan politics of today and to act in a way that I hope will gradually change the preferences of citizen and voters—not a preference for one party, but a preference for sharing ideas, and more importantly, for being able to evaluate the ideas and the methods of persuasion *as objectively as possible.*

PETULANCE

Both women and men sometimes complain about their partners being so touchy that they feel they are always walking on thin ice. Is Peter's partner Petula petulant because of something he did or didn't do, or because something else happened outside their relationship to put her in a touchy temper?

Let's assume for the moment that something negative outside their connection is niggling at Petula. What will Peter do? He does what he'd like Petula to do if *he* felt touchy because of something that happened to him—he leaves her alone. But that's not what Petula would like. She'd prefer to talk about it and hopes Peter is considerate enough to tease the details out of her.

Every relationship expert I have read or listened to (John Gray, Tony Robbins, Ellen Kreidman, Barbara deAngelis, and Alison Armstrong, among others) focuses on these kinds of gender differences. For example, the guy needs time to think it over and calm himself down, while the gal needs to talk, even while agitated, in order to sort out her thoughts. For Peter, words get in the way. For Petula, conversation clarifies.

Both would be wise to study relationship experts like those above so they can try to understand their partner *from their partner's point of view*. But it is painfully difficult for a man to think like a woman not only because he does not have a woman's chemical make up, but also because he could not have had a woman's previous experiences. And vice versa. For decades I studied material on relationships, hoping to become familiar with the multi-volume library on understanding women. Every time I thought I had sufficient insight, a new relationship surprised me with a wrinkle that made me feel incompetent enough that I had to trudge back to that multi-volume library again.

It is easy for men to cast themselves into the role of the quiet, careful reasoner while casting their female counterparts into the role of the excitable scatterbrain. But even when this is true, try switching things around. Perhaps the guy could be cast into the role of sullen loner who neglects the feelings of others, and the woman could be cast into the role of the emotionally sensitive intuitive. Why don't we consider both options? Perhaps we are not generous with our descriptions of our counterparts because, whether quiet and rational or talkative and emotive, we have no experience being anything but what we are, and it would take a dedicated and difficult effort to try to be what we are not.

From what I have read and from what I have experienced, when men consider giving the benefit of the doubt to an agitated women's emotional arguments, they feel that they will be taken advantage of. They feel that they are compromising their values and giving up their self-respect.

A. Justin Sterling in his *What Really Works with Men* writes that women, having better relationship skills from the get-go, should be the managers of the relationship. In essence, he is admitting that, as far as relationships are concerned, men are blunt objects that only a woman's skill can guide in a mutually satisfactory direction. But to do this, she has to understand men. Women traditionally have been considered more variable, more complicated, having more facets, and able to multi-task. Unfortunately, sometimes they expect the same of men. Often a women thinks that since men are far simpler than women (blunt objects compared to tapestries), she already understands them. Alison Armstrong says this is a big mistake. Armstrong says that women tend to see men as muscular, hairy women who are misbehaving, when in reality they are far more complicated—if not an entire library, perhaps a moderate-sized book collection.

In early 2020, on her FaceBook page "Understand Men", Ms. Armstrong posted a meme for the purpose of discussion that read, "Men want to help but they don't always know how. Especially when a woman is emotional. Tell him HOW he can help." When a woman is going through something either because of her man or because of outside pressures, a man often shuts down because he feels incompetent. Since his greatest reward is when he is appreciated for helping, and since he will not "play the game" unless he has a reasonable chance of succeeding, he calculates the odds of victory and then may decide to withdraw. To a woman, it may seem that he is not interested in what she is going through. Sometimes she simply would like him to hear her without offering suggestions, but he cannot feel successful doing this *unless she first tells him* that listening is what she needs, and then appreciates him for doing it.

Petulance arises in her when she feels he doesn't care. Petulance arises in him when he feels that he cannot win, so it is not worth his effort to try, and yet she expects him to do something!

ROMANTIC RELATIONSHIPS TO POLITICAL CONFLICTS

I have been using aspects of romantic relationships to help understand the arguments used in political rivalries. This may have appeared unusual, to say the least, since the two aspects of human interaction are, on the surface, quite different. In the first, people generally want to make the relationship work permanently, although they know they can end it if absolutely necessary, whereas in the second, they want to win in the short run, knowing they may not permanently rid themselves of the rivalry.

If these relationships are so different, why have pre-feminist emotional arguments, used dominantly in male-female relationships, come to dominate the political scene? Did some astute political strategist realize that these tactics could be applied to his own field or is there an underlying connection between romance and politics?

Consider romance not as dating but as marriage. Two different people with different upbringings and person-alities get together for each other's good and for the good of their family. Doesn't that describe two parties with differ-ent preferences and worldviews that come together for each other's good and for the good of their country? You may object to my describing political factions as coming together "for each other's good", but therein lays the problem: neither side sees the value in the other's point-of-view. And some-times, if one side concedes even a little, the other side takes advantage. Unfortunately, this can be a cyclical, dizzying challenge [see the next section].

In a marriage or committed relationship, disagree-ments can easily occur and occasionally one person can be surprised at the insensitivity or offensiveness displayed by the other. If one person is easily hurt, he/she will likely consider the other person insensitive and a disagreement ensues. However, if both partners have previously committed to the relationship, they put their petulance on hold in favor of understanding the other person, rather than think he/she is lacking in character or concern. In a committed relationship, concern for the relationship overrides immediate disagreements. Because each partner knows the other is committed to that same relationship, they are more likely to see the disagreement as a misunderstanding, and if it turns out not to be a misunderstanding, the disagreement can be seen as an area in which to work out a compromise.

In U.S. politics, there have been periods in which the two dominant parties either compromised or were willing to accept an opposing view because their representatives had gotten to know each other personally, and like everyday friends and co-workers whose politics differ, they got along with each other because winning wasn't the only thing. President Ronald Reagan (R) got along famously with House Speaker Tip O'Neill (D) despite their differences. President Bill Clinton (D) got along with House Speaker Newt Gingrich (R) because, to get anything done, they needed each other.

TRAPPED IN THE CYCLE

There are, however, as many examples of people

on opposite sides of the aisle that would have been happy if their opponents happened to accidentally trip into the La Brea Tar Pits. Locked in a political "marriage", opposites can get along, but it takes willingness of both parties and a commitment to the relationship (i.e. the country's well-being). As mentioned above, however, what can easily destroy harmony is one person or party lying, cheating, or clearly not caring for the wellbeing of the whole.

If Side A's exposing Side B's emotional tactics does not seem to help sway the audience, Side A may feel obliged to use emotional tactics as well. People use the guerrilla argumentation tactics on our list successfully because most people within listening range are not practiced at being objectively logical. If we all looked for and responded positively to logic and empirical proofs, emotional guerrilla tactics would not work. But as long as people continue to respond to emotion instead of logic, one party or both will use emotion exclusively in their arguments, and we will never escape the unfair guerrilla warfare cycle. We will be doomed not to negotiate or to compromise or even to test a theory, but simply to sacrifice our rational wellbeing to the side with the most passionate argument (see Chapter 16, *What If We Don't?* for more on this). In the previous section, I called this a cyclical, dizzying challenge. Now, let's step away from the whirlpool for a moment.

Let's consider something I had mentioned above: "You may object to my describing political factions as coming together 'for each other's good'." What if the side dedicated to empirical evidence used a little bit of emotionality and a great deal of consideration to help sway the odds its way. What if we try to win just a few concessions from opponents rather than trying to destroy them? What if we make them realize that we may, in fact, be in the argument "for each other's good"?

"'Becoming the opponent' means you should put yourself in an opponent's place and think from the opponent's point of view."
— Miyamoto Musashi, *The Book of Five Rings*

"If you go about dehumanizing your opponents [...] you're never going to convince them to change."   — Marushia Dark, *Thelema: Book 0 - The Fool*

"The goal in most conflicts is to destroy your opponent. The goal in apologetics is to win your opponent."   — Ravi Zacharias

"The most important tactic in an argument, next to being right, is to leave an escape hatch for your opponent so that he can gracefully swing over to your side without an embarrassing loss of face."   — Stephen Jay Gould

Chapter 8.

For Each Other's Good

It is easy to see how, in a romantic relationship, making the effort to see things from the other person's point-of-view preserves and enhances the relationship. It's not so easy to enhance the relationship (benefit the country) in a political tug-of-war in which each side cannot see the value of the other's point-of-view. But does the other side want the country to suffer just to get their way or do they believe that if things are done their way, the country will benefit and thus

even their opponents will indirectly benefit, despite themselves?

The honest answer is that often we are not really sure. And in today's world where allegedly empirical data can be manipulated so that it no longer seems to prove anything, where experts' opinions are wrong as often as amateurs' opinions, and where every amateur on the Internet thinks he/she is an expert, we are less sure than ever before. Those that argue in the parlance of petulance, claiming other people are their greatest concern, could easily be conspira-tors that simply want power for themselves.

In public debates, whether live, on radio, on TV, or recorded for the Internet, there are at least three participants, Side A, Side B, and the audience. Obviously, if Side A wins over Side B, he/she is likely to win the audience, as well, but it is more probable that both sides will go through the proce-dure of debating in order to win over the audience. Instead of making a thinly veiled appeal to the audience, what if one side treated the other as if it were attempting to come to an agreement in a business negotiation? I know that debates are not directly analogous to negotiations since in a negotia-tion both sides want to benefit themselves while still willing to benefit the other side, but that is exactly the mindset I am suggesting for political conflicts. While it is unlikely that both sides will negotiate a middle ground, it is far more likely that a sincere attempt to do so will win over the audience.

In Bob Burg's terrific book about persuasion, *Adversaries into Allies,* he suggests a five-tier approach to winning people over without manipulation or coercion:

- Control your own emotions,
- Understand the clash of belief systems,
- Acknowledge their ego,
- Set the proper frame, and
- Communicate with tact and empathy.

I won't try to condense Bob's book by going over all of these tiers in detail (besides, he discusses many more educative niceties than are relevant here), but I will note that we have already indirectly discussed #1 several times, so now I'd like to concentrate on #5 from a tripartite public debating perspective.

TACT AND EMPATHY

Lack of tact and lack of empathy has become *de rigueur* in modern political conflicts. I suspect that politeness and consideration have been victims of an increasingly less formal society and one in which, understandably, we wanted public figures to dispense with "polite" sugarcoating and "tell it like it is". Our films and TV, in an attempt to seem more true-to-life, have become cruder in their dialogue and more graphic in their sex and violence. Have films imitated life? Probably. But life imitates films as well. Whether or not you see this "realism" in entertainment as a positive development, I suspect that it has also made us less polite, less tactful, much less empathetic, and much more "in your face". Popular films, having shrugged off uptight censors of a more reserved era, indirectly give us license to be both direct and even vulgar—another sort of cyclical problem. Again, you may see only a benefit here since, in being direct, honesty comes to the fore. However, I am suggesting that under the guise of honesty, we have allowed acrimony and enmity to slip in.

When an insulted pre-feminist woman argued with her significant other, she did not concentrate on their togetherness, she was not being diplomatic, preserving his ego, or being sensitive to his feelings; rather, she was concentrating on her own feelings and trying to hurt his. His fighting fire with fire would just give her more to be angry about. His passively taking her slings and arrows might have eventually allowed her to vent, and if he understands her and is willing not to take it personally, his tolerance and inclination to endure might have eventually changed her mood sufficiently for them to discuss her issue. However, in a contemporary public debate, such passivity appears weak and void of counterarguments. Here's where fighting fire with water comes in.

Here are a few key points in maintaining a pleasant flow of cool, refreshing water when the flames of one-sided petulance appear:

(1) remain rational and relatively imperturbable,

• use facts to support your claims,

• don't take things personally, especially if there is a personal insult,

(2) understand how the opponent can feel the way he/she does,

• support the opponent's self-image/understand their good intent (even if you are not sure that they have one),

• identify a generic end goal that you both want, and

(3) suggest that, since you might be mistaken, you'd like to devise a test of both points of view (if possible over a reasonable amount of time).

BEING RATIONAL AND IMPERTURBABLE

Morihei Ueshiba, founder of Aikido, said, "Those who are skilled in combat do not become angered; those who are skilled at winning do not become afraid. Thus the wise win before the fight, while the ignorant fight to win."

Remember that you do not want to fight fire with

fire, if at all possible. Your becoming emotional or using arguments that resemble our list of pre-feminist guerrilla tactics just leaves the audience deciding which side is more emotional. You want to appear cool, calm, and collected but not condescending. You are confident because you have already marshaled the facts that support your position, so it is unlikely that your opponent will have countervailing facts. In today's world, however, one has be wary of the half-fact, the opinion from an expert, the non-argument portrayed as an argument. Your opponent may use any or all of these methods to appear as factual and as well prepared as you. Sadly, the audience is not likely to see the rhetorical chicaneries hidden by the opponent's verbal skills, so you may have to politely reveal them.

Half-facts. Anyone can look at a controversial subject and carefully select the facts that support his preferred position. Often this is done with mathematical trickery made easy by selecting certain statistics. Let's say his opinion is that there is more poverty in the USA than in the country of San Statistica. His statistics say that in San Statistica only 10 people in 100 are under their country's poverty line, while in the USA, 11.5 people in 100 are considered poor. The statistics are verifiable; however, what is left out of the statement is the location of the poverty line. In San Statistica, the average poor person makes the equivalent of $2700 a year, while in the USA, the average poor person makes $11,000 a year. But even if *those* statistics were included, the relative purchasing power of the San Statistica shilling as against the American dollar must also be weighed in. So too, must the additional benefits of government programs. If all of this were fairly calculated, one would find that the average American in poverty is as well off as the average upper middle-class person in San Statistica.

Expert opinions. If you have ever read *Wrong* by David H. Freedman, *Intellectuals and Society* by Thomas Sowell, or *The Death of Expertise* by Tom Nichols, you realize that the term "expert" may not represent what we commonly think it does. Whenever a debate opponent cites an expert opinion, note to him that opinions are not facts, nor even half-facts, then ask for the data from which the opinion was drawn. Seldom do opponents have access to that data; rather they depend on trusted "experts", who already agree with them, to make their points. You can then suggest it would be quite educative to hear your opponent's expert discuss opinions with an expert that disagrees with him.

Non-arguments. These are methods by which debaters cleverly avoid engaging in the actual issues they claim to be engaged in. They vary from *ad hominem* accusations (attacking the opponent rather than the argument) to claims that evidence is not proof as if evidence did not at least count toward a proof (What else but evidence would count toward a proof?) to saying something about a related argument that says nothing about the argument at hand, etc.

YOU: Historically, the minimum wage was meant to set a bargaining "bottom line" so that employers could not offer lower and lower wages in an employer's market, in order to take advantage of potential employees' ignorance of what other potential employees would work for. Minimum wage was never meant as a living wage. When you raise the minimum wage, you give the employer a disincentive to hire inexperienced help so that fewer entry-level jobs are available. This flies against the original purpose of the minimum wage—to protect the inexperienced worker.

OPPONENT: So you want inexperienced workers not to earn a living at all! They don't work just so your precious employer can put more money in his own pocket!

YOU: If the employer cannot hire people at a wage she can afford for a job she needs done, using the marketplace to determine what a certain job is worth, then fewer people will be employed and the business will be less efficient, eventually making less money for the employer, thus prohibiting the expansion of a business that would eventually hire more people.

OPPONENT: Right. Expand the business while the worker is kept at a minimum wage so that the employer can make more and more money. Why do you hate the poor so much?

YOU: Could it be that you hate the employer who helps the poor by offering them jobs? Are you saying that you do not want to see poor people employed?

OPPONENT: Of course not! I just want to see them employed at higher wages.

YOU: I know. So do I, so let's get them jobs first.

UNDERSTANDING THE OPPONENT

Besides doing your homework before a debate by reviewing articles or books the opponent has written and by watching or listening to previous interviews, you should also get a sense of the opponent's sincerity. Some people have taken up a specific viewpoint because they have stood for certain principles for a long time. Others have become champions of a viewpoint because they are facile at making emotional arguments and have gained acclaim from their comrades by using those arguments successfully. In other words, appealing to their group is more important to them than the viewpoint itself. If their party or their cause shifted what it stood for, they would defend that new position because they gain ego-satisfaction from their team, rather than their being committed to a principle. Political parties and niche groups have been known to suddenly reverse their positions as soon as their opponents seem to be more successful in defending those positions. In other words, they would rather hold status in a community than hold steady to a position. They would rather fight for a self-contradictory point-of-view than join the opposing party.

In any confrontation, egos are on the line. If you can preserve your opponent's ego while winning the audience, the audience will appreciate you even more.

YOU: If I understand you correctly, you believe that it is the government's role to provide guaranteed healthcare to all its citizens. Is that correct?

OPPONENT: Yes, healthcare is a right. My goal is to have healthcare for everyone.

YOU: And you also think that being able to earn a living is a right, is that also correct?

OPPONENT: Of course, one should be able to earn a living, but if one cannot earn a living, one should not be allowed to slip through the cracks, suffer, and die.

YOU: You might be surprised to learn that I agree with your goals. They seem to come from a caring person who would hate to see anyone suffer.

OPPONENT: Exactly. There is enough misery in the world without our adding to it by not alleviating suffering wherever possible.

YOU: I don't believe that alleviating an apparent problem in one area and creating it in another can be considered 'caring'. Do you?

OPPONENT: That depends. What do you mean?

YOU: What if we discovered that guaranteed healthcare destroys jobs, lowers the income of the health worker, and makes medical care less accessible, as well?

OPPONENT: National healthcare might put a dent in the income of Big Pharma, but I doubt if it will destroy any other jobs.

YOU: Although I share your doubts about the value of some Big Pharma actions, that industry employs a lot of people. Also, the drugs it produces and the equipment the medical industry produces, obviously for a profit, are essential to those other countries that already have national healthcare. Those countries depend on our free market innovations, the market's gradually lowering prices, and the market's increasing the availability of drugs and equipment. They depend on our market-based healthcare system to help people in their countries—countries where free medical care is often overwhelmed, where wait-times are long, and where innovations would not exist were it not for our inefficient market-based system.

OPPONENT: It's fine for you to say Big Pharma and other medical industries contribute something to the medical field, but that doesn't mean they don't rip off patients directly or through insurance costs. Limiting profits by law helps the consumer afford medicines and treatment.

YOU: For a time, perhaps, but it also makes those products scarcer since no one has the incentive to produce them or market them. Okay, I can

understand your concern. But I think you may agree that we also don't want to give up medical innovations, dissuade students from entering the medical profession, or sacrifice the quality of healthcare.
It wouldn't be any good if our tax burden were to increase to pay for national healthcare only to see the quality of our medical services decrease.

OPPONENT: You have no evidence to support the idea that under national healthcare that would happen.

YOU: Only the evidence from other countries. Since you are a caring person, I would suggest spreading that concern in a wider arc, caring not only for those who need healthcare, but also those who provide it, and the quality and availability of what they provide. Maybe we can come up with a modified system in which the government's role is not universal and the resulting care is still maximal. It's quite a challenge. What do you say?

In forming your argument this way, you are attempting to make an ally of your adversary and the audience realizes that his refusal would portray a stubborn "my way or the highway" attitude.

SUGGESTING A TEST

Often arguments are reduced to predictions about the future. For decades, I have heard people say that some government program is not an expense but an investment. Sounds good, but ten or twenty years later, when little or no benefit occurs because of the program, the expense is still there. Any reasonable person, whether on the Left or on the Right, would reject pouring good money after bad and simultaneously not obtaining the expected result. And yet government waste is rampant. If only we had been able to test the proposed program before implementing it!

So when an opponent predicts a future outcome (if only everyone will support his point of view), ask if he would be willing to design an experiment to see if the outcome he predicts will likely come true. If he agrees, the argument's resolution can be deferred until after the experiment has been designed, agreed upon by both parties, and applied. If he is unwilling to participate, that suggests to the audience that he is more interested in accruing support for his vision rather than having his vision produce the desired result.

In each of these suggested methods of debating an opponent, who is likely to be emotional and use guerrilla tactics, you are trying to attain harmony with both the opponent and the audience, making it clear that you want what is good for everyone. It is up to the opponent to concur with this intention. If he does not, it will at least be clear to the audience that you have everyone's wellbeing in mind.

Sometimes, the opponent is both stubborn and nasty and needs to be disciplined. To do so as if you were the Lord of the Universe comes across as just a little bit pretentious, but not to do so comes across as weak-willed or cowardly. Is there a balanced way to strike back when you feel it is necessary?

Chapter 9.

Counterpunching

PREMATURE CONDEMNATIONS

Although women can be guilty of spousal abuse, men commit far greater number of offenses. This is especially egregious because men are generally larger and stronger. Size and strength are the most obvious inequalities between the genders. Physical power is less important for equality in the modern world where intelligence and drive dominates, but in situations where a verbally less skilled male loses his temper and acts out physically, the physical inequality rears its (ugly) head. I would suggest that even Gloria Steinem would recognize this inequality and object to a man's applying superior physical power as well as objecting to his alleg-edly less developed rage control.

Does the male really have less rage control or are people more tolerant of female rage because women are less likely to strike out or to harm their male partners if they do? I am not hazarding a guess here, rather I want to emphasize that having equal rights, equal pay, and equal respect is not the same as having equal attributes, and that advocating for equality cannot possibly mean advocating for identity. Given this fact, it is obvious both that women would be wise to learn how to protect themselves, and more importantly, that men learn not to revert to violence simply because they have difficulty arguing their way out of a crazy kitchen quarrel about who clipped the last chip.

While I was driving a female friend home, we passed a local farm stand and I asked if she would like to stop to buy anything. She said that she would not shop there since she had heard on the police scanner than the owner had been arrested the night before during a domestic disturbance. I understood why she might not want to shop there. "It would be interesting to find out the details," I said. "I wonder what set him off."

"It doesn't matter," she said, "there is no excuse for striking a woman!"

First, neither of us knew if the woman of the house had been struck. Second, although my friend would never admit it, there is indeed an excuse for a man to strike a woman—the same excuse a man has in striking another man: to protect himself. It might be statistically unlikely that a woman would lash out physically, but it is not un-heard of that an angry wife, feeling she could not physically overcome her husband, might draw a knife. Third, although the man is responsible for controlling his own temper, and certainly for not initiating violence, I have known of situa-tions in which the woman goaded the man into acting out, wrong as he may have been to do so, in order to get him into trouble. I have also known of more than one situation in which a woman reported her significant other to the police, claiming that he struck her when he did not.

I had not been implying to my friend that the woman was the aggressor in the domestic disturbance situation or that somehow the husband was not culpable; rather, I wanted to know the details of the conflict in order to better understand what went wrong in their "negotiations". But my friend would not hear of it. He was absolutely wrong, and that was that.

Any bully, any tyrant, or anyone at all who takes advantage of superior size and strength, meanness, or force of arms in an attempt to intimidate and physically debilitate a less capable opponent, is in my opinion the lowest of the low and should thank their lucky stars that I am not a judge hearing their case. However, because I believe in equal rights under the law, I cannot assume a person is a tyrant who bullies others simply because he is male or because a friend thinks no opinion other than "guilty" is admissible.

I have another friend, a petite but nonetheless tough woman, who spent most of her adult life teaching women how to deal with a physical assault. She began her public career as a teacher in the Model Mugging program in which a man dresses up in a heavily padded uniform and badmouths and then manhandles a female student to the point where it is appropriate to let herself go and beat the holy bejeebers out of him (hence the need for the suit). Later in life, my friend gave workshops and lectures on assertiveness and self-defense. For her romantic relationships she likes men, but because of personal experiences, she is especially sensitive to men that take advantage of women who have been drinking at parties or at a bar.

In response to a well-publicized sexual assault charge, my friend posted on her Facebook account, "Believe The Victim!" Those that did not agree with her were asked to delete their friendship status immediately. This angry exhortation had, without hearing any evidence, immediately characterized the woman in the news story as a victim, thus not only characterizing the man as the assailant, but also convicting him. It would be one thing if the woman in question had stumbled into the police station, bruised and in shock, but this specific accusation was 20 years old and had been initially reported only to a girlfriend, who did not remember the report! My friend believed that women simply don't lie about these things, so if the purported victim says she had been a victim, it must have been the truth, even though her corroborating evidence was not verifiable and even though the alibi of the accused man was.

A third female friend also believed the woman's charge because when she had been working at a restaurant 40 years before, the male proprietor had pinned her to the wall and made sexual advances. "How," I asked, "does your account have anything to do with this news story?" "It just goes to show," she said, "that men do these things." This very intelligent, well-educated woman would have bristled if I had made generic negative claims about women, but she had no problem making them about men. She was not a sexist, but she was functioning from an emotionally biased point of view.

How can three mature, intelligent, experienced women assume the worse of a man without knowing the facts? I suspect that these are examples of Alison Armstrong's "rage monster" in a public setting. None of my friends were using pre-feminist guerrilla *tactics* to make their arguments, but all were "taking something out of context" (since they did not know the context), "jumping to extreme conclusions", "mind reading", and "never admitting they could be wrong".

How does this fold over into political arguments?

POLITICAL PARALLELS

I recently saw a roundtable discussion on TV regarding the potential of voter fraud, certainly an important issue to either side of the aisle. One guest (Party A) was saying that a lot of the controversy would be alleviated if only jurisdictions culled their voting lists regularly. The opposing guest (Party B) implied that this was racist since she feared that "culling" was a code for taking black voters off the list. She said that she knew a number of cases where blacks that had not voted for several cycles returned to the polls to find their name had been expunged.

Of course, the very mention of "racism" sets off emotional sirens so that the atmosphere of the discussion or debate suddenly becomes impassioned. Although Party B did not use the term directly, her concern (and I believe it was genuine) that certain voters would not be able to exercise their rights because of their skin color supercharged the atmosphere. By implying racism, she was "jumping to an extreme conclusion" as well as "mind reading".

Party A then argued that "culling voter lists" means exactly that—when voters do not vote after a certain number of elections, their name is removed and they would have to register again to have it reappear on the voter lists. Technically, Mr. A was correct, but I think his argument was not only unsatisfying to Ms. B, but also would not easily win over an audience. He was being factual, but missed an opportunity to show Ms. B's emotional bias as well as to offer an alternative that might be satisfying to all three parties.

Consider an alternative approach. Party A could have said, "While I agree that we have to be as careful of fraud in culling lists as we do in counting votes, it should be known that names do not have an obvious race. When people cull a list, unless they know everyone in town, a John Smith could be black or white, so it is unlikely that there is racial targeting when lists are kept current. We would, however, have to make sure that all voters appreciate how many election cycles they can miss before they have to reregister. By culling regularly, we prevent deceased voters names being used for illegal votes. And I'm sure neither of us wants dead people voting." In this way, he would have been sensitive to Party B's concerns while still showing the validity of his viewpoint.

SLIP AND JAB

In boxing, the jab is a relatively weak punch, but it is annoying and can set the opponent up for more powerful blows. If you slip the opponent's jab and counter with your own, it can really take the opponent by surprise.

When a debate opponent does not seem to appreciate your trying to offer him/her an out, does not see that "for each other's good" may be the best for both parties in the discussion, or continues to use guerrilla tactics to emotionally sway the audience, you may have to slip and jab.

A boxer may slip, jab, and then back off, if he is still "feeling out" his opponent, but he also may follow up with a combination while the opponent is temporarily stung. In a discussion where the audience can be won over, I prefer to slip, jab, and back off with a smile, letting both the opponent and the audience know that I can play at his game, too, but prefer not to.

Slip, jab, and smile. When Abraham Lincoln was accused of being two-faced, he said, "If I were two-faced, would I be wearing this one?" Some quick additional examples come to mind, from both President Kennedy and President Reagan.

Kennedy had been accused of allowing his father to buy his election. Instead of opposing the accusation, he made light of it. Pretending to read a telegram from his father he said, "Dear Jack: Don't buy a single vote more than necessary. I'll be damned if I'm going to pay for a landslide. Love, Dad." After being elected, Kennedy was criticized for choosing his 35-year-old brother, Robert, as Attorney General of the United States. Said the president: "I don't see anything wrong with giving Bobby a little legal experience before he goes out on his own to practice law." (*From NPR.org.*)

Candidate Reagan was prepared for his 1984 opponent Walter Mondale's criticism of his age. He famously said, "I want you to know that…I will not make age an issue of this campaign. I am not going to exploit, for political purposes, my opponent's youth and inexperience." Even Mondale laughed. Criticized for taking naps during the workday, Reagan said, "I never drink coffee at lunch. I find it keeps me awake for the afternoon." Without getting into the pros or cons of the abortion debate, Reagan made his point with humor (in an area where humor is seldom possible): "I've noticed that everyone who is for abortion has already been born." (*From Liveabout.com.*)

Must one use humor while delivering a jab? Probably not; but it certainly helps to be self-effacing. An audience is more likely to respond positively to a good-natured jab than to a sneaky cheap shot. The difference between the two is that the first uses humor and a sincere "we're in this together" attitude.

DONCHA THINK?

I think most political discussions would benefit from the assumption that "what benefits me actually also benefits you", even if a jab has to be thrown in the cases where opponents use emotional rhetoric.

Questions like: "Aren't you concerned at all that blacks are not allowed vote because of your attempt to clean up voter lists? Doesn't that trouble you in the least?" are inelegant attempts to create *ad hominem* arguments that essential imply, "Since I know my position is virtuous, yours cannot be." It assumes (a) that my point of view is objectively true (in this case, that blacks are being denying voting rights), (b) that your point of view is the reason this travesty is occurring, and (c) that since it is obvious that voter rights cannot morally be removed, you must be immoral. The initial punch attempted to follow up with more powerful body blows. If left unchallenged, the emotional impact of such questions can win an audience that is not attuned to sorting out tactical slight of hand.

How can the unfeeling, potentially racist, clearly immoral guest respond? Will a slip and jab be enough? It might be enough if delivered with Kennedy- or Reagan-style humor and a suggestion that the opposition already agrees with the counter viewpoint: "I want every legal voter, regardless of race or background, to have an opportunity to vote. That would be the ethical thing to do, don't you think? We have found that in several elections, even those voters who have passed away have managed to cast a ballot. Most of the voters in this city are white. It would be immoral if more deceased white voters cast ballots than deceased black voters, don't you think?"

GIVE-AND-TAKE or GOING WITH THE FLOW

The strategy (whether planned or incidental) behind the petulant guerrilla rhetoric is to completely dominate the argument so that the other side has no chance to contend. Those that use such a strategy expect their opponents to attempt to defend themselves and sometimes fight back wildly, but they do not expect to be counterpunched.

Alison Armstrong suggests that, although it seems unfair to apologize when the man has done nothing wrong (from his own point of view), the man's sincere apology is the only thing that can tame the woman's rage monster. This is a very hard thing for him to do since honor tells him he should never pretend to be sorry for anything for which he is not truly sorry. It goes against his personal pride and he also feels that she, who remembers everything, would bring his apology up again as proof that he is a bad boy and that she was right. Yet Ms. Armstrong is suggesting that he never counterpunch. To her credit, Ms. Armstrong also suggests that women should never take advantage of his apology by holding it over his head as proof that she is always right, but instead be grateful that he values the relationship so much that he is willing to chance his honor to relieve her anxiety and anger. She suggests, in other words, that the woman appreciate his not counterpunching.

But in a personal debate with a political rival, as we have suggested above, sometimes counterpunching is necessary to prove to both your opponent and also to your audience that you are a worthy rival. The Give-and-take in boxing or karate is like the Slip and Jab in that it can take an opponent by surprise, but the method is somewhat different. Give-and-take makes it look like you are taking a non-combative, even a submissive route, but you are not.

In "soft" martial arts like Judo or Aikido, the initial

reception of an attack feels submissive, both to the attacker and to the defender, but the defender's intention is to let the attacker overextend himself until he is off-balanced and susceptible to a counterattack (in our case, this would be much less devastating than a lock, takedown, blow, or throw), but it would still be recognized both by the attacker and by witnesses (the audience) as a counterattack.

Let's assume your opponent is using the following tactics:

- **Jumping to extreme conclusions/actions,**
- **Mind reading,**
- **Drawing conclusions based on facts that could have other interpretations,**
- **Assuming that the opposite party means something they may not mean, and**
- **Since I know I am virtuous, you cannot be.**

OPPONENT: Since businesses want to employ workers at low wages in order to increase their profits, it stands to reason that undocumented immigrants will fill that need.

YOU: Actually, I think you are making a valid point and would like to hear you flesh it out.

OPPONENT: When you say that we should employ Americans before employing immigrants, you are saying that Americans are somehow better than they. If you simply left the immigrants to work here in peace, they would pay taxes and add to the success of the economy.

YOU: Aren't you afraid that employers will offer them lower wages than the current market demands?

OPPONENT: You suggest that immigrants will "bid the wages down" because you are afraid that fewer Americans will have jobs.

YOU: I think we can agree on that point.

OPPONENT: But businesses will make more money, expand, and will be able to employ more Americans after a time. That's what you always say. Since you are so employer-friendly, your only reason for not wanting undocumented immigrants to work is because you are racist enough to think that their lives are not worth a paycheck.

YOU: I see. And your argument that favors illegal aliens over Americans is, of course, far from racially biased. And yet, you have illegals working at the low wages that you normally oppose as unconscionable for citizens of this country, and citizens of this country not working at all.

HELP HIM/HER OUT

Bob Beckel was a former host of *Off the Record* on CBS, a political analyst, and a Democratic operative. Tony Snow was a former host of *Fox News Sunday* and a former press secretary for President George W. Bush. They had also co-hosted *Crossfire* on CNN. Although they seemed to possess quite different personalities as well as political points of view, they were friends.

Snow died from cancer in 2008. When Beckel was asked about Snow, he told a story about a time that they were staying in a hotel, scheduled to deliver contrasting addresses the next morning. Bob had not written his speech before having fallen asleep somewhat inebriated. When Bob awoke just in time to leave for the event, he discovered that Tony had written his speech for him *from Beckel's point of view*! Snow could have procured an easy victory by letting Beckel sweat during his speech in an attempt to extemporaneously cover his lack of preparation, but Snow was a better person than that. As a result of Snow's integrity, the audience heard two contrasting points of view.

In the short run, Snow sacrificed an easy win. In the long run, however, he won both Beckel's and his fellow journalists' respect. He neither slipped and jabbed, nor went with the flow. Dedicated to the fair presentation of ideas, his counterpunch was more of a helping hand.

Chapter 10.

The First Move & Other Counters

"Oh sure!" you say, "It's all well and good to have clever tactical methods to deal with people's emotional rhetoric, but that's not going to change their ways! It is beyond annoying to read half-logical, subtly emotional Facebook memes or hear similarly emotional partisan expressions repeated in daily life, and not be able to correct the twisted reasoning behind them. It would take too long and people wouldn't pay attention anyway!"

True. I completely agree. But someone has to start rebalancing the scales. You have just read about half of this book. Let's say you completely agree with it and are thrilled that someone has put much of your thinking into writing. Does its mere publication mean that suddenly the culture will be imbued with a new impetus toward rational thinking, rational argumentation, and fairness to the other side? Occasionally, there are books that shake up the culture, but generally, if a book makes a mark at all, it will be a small one. Will people with whom you disagree even read this book? That's unlikely, even if you specifically recommend it. However, those who need some reinforcement, some articulation of what they already believe, might just take your recommendation to give the book a try. Further, those who often think logically, but are as swayed as the rest of the culture toward accepting emotional arguments, might consider reading it. Small victories are better than no victories.

Change happens slowly. Sometimes it swings one direction and then another before finding a balance. We did not become an emotionally sensitive culture overnight. Nor did we become a logically inept culture overnight. Pendulums may run out of momentum, but they do not stop on command.

PATIENCE IS ANNOYING

As Lao Tsu said, "A journey of a thousand miles begins with a single step." Patience is annoying, but it is still a virtue. Unfortunately, people confuse patience with inaction or passivity. I would rather think of patience as active self-restraint and/or a refusal to over-react. The thousand-mile journey takes patience, but that does not mean it is passive.

Just as I do not advocate an emotional approach to discussions, debates, or any sort of argumentation, I would not advocate an impatient approach to changing the culture. It is precisely the impatient approach that submits to coaxing others passionately rather than convincing them rationally. Both can persuade, but using rational argumentation takes effort, thus it is slower. Effort, after all, can be annoying. Why do I favor the more effortful method then? Because I believe it is superior in producing a cultural interchange that is more likely to relate to reality.

Winning debates or emerging as the favorite in a discussion can, of course, be valuable, but sometimes there is simply no way to win or, more importantly, no way to make your winning influential enough to change the culture you are aiming to change. Our current Western culture has become both disrespectful and intolerant. Partially, this is because the "other guys" have become disrespectful and intolerant. Damn that other guy! Because patience can be very annoying, because tolerance can wear thin, and because turning the other cheek can result in multiple contusions, the most rational of debaters can also react disrespectfully. Yet doing battle against the opponents' emotional tactics by using emotional tactics will not eliminate emotional tactics.

Or will it?

MA! HE'S PICKING ON ME!

Remember that in many political interchanges, there are at least three parties: you, your opponent, and an audience. In cases where you are discussing politics one-on-one, your opposite number can also act like an audience, albeit an unconscious audience, but still evaluating the effectiveness of what you are saying and how you are saying it.

If rational discourse, clever comebacks, and a pleasant attitude toward your opponent seem not to be convincing the audience that emotionality is unproductive, perhaps exaggerating your emotionality in a humorous way can make the audience aware of what is really going on.

OPPONENT: You must admit that there is income inequality in The United States, which is the surface manifestation of a systemic racism and sexism.

YOU: I certainly agree to the income inequality part. I am sure you earn more money than I.

OPPONENT: No, I mean a disparity in income because of race or gender.

YOU: But we are the same race and gender! Why are you paid more than I am?

OPPONENT: Get serious! I am talking about women earning less than men and Blacks earning less than Whites.

YOU: I met Shaquille O'Neal once. He earns more in retirement than I earned in my best year of employment—maybe even more than you. But you may be right about the inequality thing. He is, after all, not a woman.

OPPONENT: This is a serious problem. Your joking around means you are not serious about addressing it.

YOU: I will be happy to address any serious problem seriously.

OPPONENT: Well? Go ahead. Say something.

YOU: Okay. Yes, there is income inequality between most individuals.

OPPONENT: And Blacks and women are on the lower end of the scale, so obviously the cultural is full of endemic racism and sexism.

YOU: But you make more than I and Shaquille makes more than you!

OPPONENT: You are talking about individuals. I am talking about generic categories.

YOU: A generic category does not have an income. Only individuals have incomes. I have a friend who makes way more than both of us because she is a lawyer.

OPPONENT: That's fine, but generally women earn less per year than men.

YOU: In what category?

OPPONENT: In general.

YOU: "In general" doesn't exist. No one is employed in general. Everyone has a job description in one field or another. Are you telling me that you want everyone to be employed in general so that no one has a specific job?

OPPONENT: Don't be absurd! Once again, you are making fun of a situation that proves the existence of both racism and sexism. Obviously, these things don't matter to you as long as Whites and men make more money than Blacks and women.

YOU: Obviously, you do not wish to compare statistics in one field, but would rather imply bias instead of analyzing facts. That means that facts don't matter to you as long as you can imply your opponent is a racist or sexist. That's not fair! I want my mommy!

OPPONENT: Is she the one who taught you to be such a baby?

YOU: Me am a baby racist and sexist. Me want my mommy!

OPPONENT: Mr. Moderator, I think this discussion is turning into a comedy act. Can you please ask my opponent to stay on the subject?

YOU: You mean the subject is not calling each other names? Sorry, I didn't know.

OPPONENT: I didn't call you a name! I am merely suggesting that income inequality is evidence of discrimination in this country and that you don't seem to mind at all.

YOU: Racism and sexism would bother me. Income inequality, not so much. If you'll provide us with statistics that measure the income of Blacks vs. Whites or women vs. men in the same profession, with same amount of experience, in the same geographical area, during the same time periods, having worked the same number of hours on projects of similar value, and they turn out to be grossly unequal, I might join you in seeking a redress of grievances. But, as of right now, you are not providing enough information to be convincing except to those who already want to believe your point of view. More detailed information might keep us from trying to make a system appear prejudiced when, in almost every case, individual people are compensated fairly.

OPPONENT: You don't know what you're talking about!

YOU: I know, I'm pitifully ignorant. That's why I'd like you to enlighten me. Mama, he keeps picking on me! I'll bet it's because I am a white male and therefore must be racist and sexist. Whatcha think?

Of course, any method can be overdone and this one is especially susceptible to audience disapproval. It is important that, before using such an ironic strategy, that your opponent has made obvious that he/she is more interested in putting you down than in raising the truth.

INTERCEPTING

Another anti-guerrilla tactic: in Japanese karate, it is called *sen-no-sen* (literally, "initiative of initiative"). I call it Intercepting. When you are familiar with the opponent's tactics and know when the opponent is about to strike, let him initiate then strike quickly enough so that you make contact first.

> OPPONENT: With all the evidence out there, you would think that the government would do something about global warming.
>
> YOU: Would you prefer to regulate more, or tax more?
>
> OPPONENT: I think we need both!
>
> YOU: How would we regulate China and India? Or tax them, for that matter?
>
> OPPONENT: Well, obviously, we couldn't, so….
>
> YOU: So we'll need to tax citizens of this country and then what? Give it to the Chinese and Indians to help with their carbon footprint or their pollution of the oceans?
>
> OPPONENT: That might be the only way to….
>
> YOU: How could you assure that they would spend that money on cutting pollution?
>
> OPPONENT: We'd have to take care of business at home first.
>
> YOU: Great. So we'll create more regulation and higher taxes on the economy that produces the least pollution so that we can hand over taxpayer dollars to the countries that create the most.
>
> OPPONENT: This is why I Have always ad-

vocated a one-world government. That way, global problems…

YOU: …will be everyone's problems. Instead of sharing problems, why don't we simply share solutions? If we explain what the lowest polluting large economy is doing right, it will be up the other countries to follow suit, if they really care about the problem as you see it. If they don't care, then either the problems isn't as bad as you wish to believe or they are just waiting for us to do all the heavy lifting.

THE FIRST MOVE

This tactic is a variation of the above tactic. In karate, it would be referred to simply as *sen* (initiative). You attack first. But the trick, in this case, is to attack with the opponent's own theme and have him/her oppose your exaggerated version of it.

YOU: I think we should all be on the side of any black man who dies because of police brutality.

OPPONENT: Yes! People are protesting the recent shooting of a black man by taking to the streets.

YOU: I know. They are even looting. Yay! Free stuff will help us correct racial injustice!

OPPONENT: A dream deferred explodes, as Langston Hughes said.

YOU: I know, I want to help. Is there a local window I can break?

OPPONENT: How does that help?

YOU: Precisely.

I know, I know, tactics can be wearisome and it annoys you even to have to be tactical when it would be so much easier if everyone were just rational—or at least fair—or at least willing to listen. But, noooo. So argumentation through petulance continues and will continue until it reaches a tipping point. That tipping point will be when the audience recognizes it and grows tired of it.

USE YOUR OWN BUMPER STICKER LOGIC

One of the byproducts of arguing from emotion is that one can elicit an emotion with a photo or a short phrase without regard to fleshing out or giving empirical evidence for an argument. We used to see these kinds of arguments on bumper stickers. Now they appear most often in memes. Political figures and news commentators use bumper sticker arguments in the form of sound bites. When the concise phrase seems to elicit the desired emotion, it becomes popular so that no one questions it or the ideas behind it.

Social Justice. Who can argue with justice in society? No one. However, if you notice that the phrase "social justice" has gone without a strict definition and has been used to mean "a correction for income inequality", you might want to find out if the person or group using the phrase suggests a reason for that inequality. Some say racism or sexism accounts for income inequality. Others do not talk about equal treatment under the law, but aspire to equal results for all, i.e. social equity. Depending on what they mean when they use the social justice phrase, you may think twice about supporting every claim that employs it. However, because there is no single definition of the term, there is no simple inversion of the term.

You cannot advocate Private Justice since that would be vigilantism. You cannot advocate Social Injustice since makes you sound like you do not want people to have better incomes or that you do not want the equal application of justice for all. You want a succinct phrase that emphasizes justice that is fairly applied, without implying that differences between individuals are somehow evil. I personally like "Freedom from Forced Equality", "Freedom from Artificial Fairness", or "Liberty to Improve", but perhaps you can come up with something even more succinct and descriptive.

Black Lives Matter. One of the cleverest and most successful phrases is the name for the anti-police-violence group Black Lives Matter. The instant implication that everyone intuits is that, to some people, black lives do not matter. Not to care about a life because of a skin tone is obviously unjust and racist. Thus, the BLM phrase starts with all reasonable people agreeing with the sentiment. If you do not think black lives matter, then you are likely a racist. So far so good.

Later you discover that the incident that sparked the formation of BLM, where allegedly the police gunned down an unarmed black man surrendering with his hands up, was not objectively reported. Several eyewitnesses, some of whom were black, said that Michael Brown had tried to take Officer Wilson's gun, and after being chased and stopped, rushed the policeman. An FBI investigation found no evidence to suggest that Brown had his hands up and was saying, "Don't shoot," as subsequent protestors claimed. (For details, see Wikipedia article: *https://en.wikipedia.org/ wiki/Shooting_of_Michael_Brown*).

But there have been plenty of other incidences where police reacted improperly and black people were killed. Therefore, the spirit of BLM is completely valid. Although you may have doubts about just how systemic racism in America is, you certainly stand for appropriate police ac- tion—not an overreaction based on the race of an alleged perpetrator.

Now you learn that anarchist groups have infiltrated some BLM chapters, using race to shield themselves against accusations of anti-American activity, and later you learn that BLM leaders have admitted to being Marxists. You are not anti-American, nor are you an anarchist, but you cannot exactly say, "Black lives don't matter," and yet you want to stand against police brutality without standing for an unrelated cause. What would be an accurate modified sentiment of the BLM phrase?

You cannot say, "White Lives Matter." Although obviously true, that would seem to imply that *only* white lives matter, which seems racist. Wait! That's not fair. Why doesn't the Black Lives Matter slogan imply only black lives matter? Why does it not seem racist? Obviously, it is because cops are not threatening white lives. But statistically, cops are at least 25% more likely to shoot white perpetrators than black. So what verbal formulation could respectfully argue against an obviously accurate phrase like Black Lives Matter?

I've seen a headline that read, "Black Lies Matter", but no matter what the content of the concomitant article, the headline itself is one-sided and, even if meant to suggest a need to find the truth, it does not address your concerns.

How about the currently popular "All Lives Matter"? But that phrase has been attacked for skirting the original issue of police brutality against blacks by implying lives that are in danger don't matter more, at least right away. A friend of mine in Texas published an excellent video meme, that I believe was intended to explain why BLM advocates don't want to accept the ALM idea. Woman B is rushing to help put out a burning house. Woman A says, "What about my house?"

Woman B: "But your house isn't on fire."

Woman A: "But all houses matter."

It was very effective, as are many emotionally laden memes, and hard to argue against. It emotionally conveyed an attitude without using slurs and without using race itself. Yay. But emotional memes keep one from thinking more deeply, so I thought for a while. We don't know who is in or who owns the burning house. Of course, because it is "on fire", it needs attention just as a cop unjustifiably killing a black suspect would need attention (the 2020 police killing of George Floyd is the most obvious example.). Ironically, however, when the same thing happens to a white suspect (and it has), it is ignored (lookup the 2016 police killing of Tony Timpa, a mirror image of Floyd's killing).

The ALM slogan tries to keep the concern non-racial, while the BLM slogan intends to point out the racial concern. To BLM advocates, the ALM slogan takes away from their point. To the ALM advocate, it isn't just black lives that could be endangered.

I understand both points of view, as well as the burning house analogy; however, that analogy can take so many twists and turns (who lit the fire? who tries to put it out? who has added gasoline? what if the house was blue? etc.) that when really examined, it fails to address the entire issue. Unfortunately, fires can only be investigated when they are out. Meanwhile, if one wants to rail against police misconduct without making it racial, what emotional phrase could one use?

Whether you like or dislike the BLM movement, you have to acknowledge the power of its Bumper Sticker Logic, and the difficulty one finds in opposing aspects of a movement that employs such a powerful name. The best Bumper Sticker counterargument I have seen so far is, "Innocent Lives Matter": it has the advantage of being non-racial, cutting to the core of the problem, and still supporting legitimate police work.

Are there other emotionally powerful bumper sticker phrases that can be countered with equally effective bumper sticker phrases?

My Body, My Choice. Another well-formulated protest poster is the reproductive rights phrase "My Body, My Choice". Everyone agrees that an individual controls his/her own body. How can you say otherwise? You certainly do not want the state to determine what you do with your body, and you even support Roe v. Wade's tripartite division of when abortions should be considered legal, but you have no-ticed that those who are protesting *for* "reproductive rights" have already achieved the Roe vs. Wade decision and now wish to extend that right into late-term abortion—abortion during the last trimester that Roe vs. Wade holds as unac-ceptable. How can you argue with the succinct and emotion-ally powerful phrase, "My Body, My Choice" yet make an exception for late-term abortion? One counter is to use the same phrase, add a question mark and a picture of an unborn child. As a visual meme this would be emotionally powerful, but as a phrase, it is not sufficiently different to engage the imagination.

If you support voluntary abortions during the first trimester, but definitely not in the third trimester, you could emphasize the responsibilities of the mother by saying, "Make a Choice Before the Baby has a Body."

If you are a pro-lifer (supporting no abortions after conception, rather than the Roe v. Wade divisions), you can say, ***"Baby Bodies Have No Choice."***

Stop Pretending Your Racism Is Patriotism. I believe this phrase was originally intended as an "all Mus-lims are not jihadists" jibe. The initial emotional response is stimulated by two words heavily laden with historical impli-cations: racism and patriotism. It is obvious that racism and patriotism are two different subjects, so the sentence captures our attention in that it implies that some people confuse the two. A moment's reflection would tell you that a patriot could be harboring a racist attitude. However, if you dwell on the phrase, it is also clear that to really support the ideals of the USA (i.e. freedom and justice for all) means you cannot also act like a racist. This one is difficult to counter since you want only Patriotism to apply. To oppose it, therefore, you would have to say, "I'm not a racist, but I am a patriot!", a phrase that is too defensive and negative to be counter-aggressive. Tricky things, these Bumper Sticker phrases, eh? To be positive and straightforward, you might say, ***"Patriotism Means Being Anti-racism"***.

No Human Is Illegal. In an attempt to defend "undocumented immigrants" crossing the southern U.S. border illegally, this phrase calls upon a U.S. citizen's natural tendency to (a) support equal rights, and (b) to support the law and avoid illegalities. It circumnavigates the issue of illegal immigration by deflecting one's attention to the common humanity of people, who, when in dire straits, break the law. The easy counter phrase is ***"Humans Aren't Illegal, but Human Actions Can Be"***; however, that is long and not emotionally stirring. Stronger and more to the point might be something like ***"No Illegal Action is Humane"***.

ADMIT WHEN YOU ARE/WERE WRONG

Even if you are skilled in rational counterarguments and emotional counter-tactics, you can find yourself mistaken either in a detail or in your summary position. Your trustworthiness is enhanced whenever you admit you had wrong information, made a wrong judgment, or came to a wrong conclusion.

Being skilled at defanging emotional arguments helps to deal with the petulant opponent, but your attitude is important as well, as we discuss in the next chapter.

Chapter 11.

Reality Should Be the Referee

IS RATIONALITY REALLY SUPERIOR?

My response to this question is, "Superior to what and in which context?" Those who love emotion often think that accepting a sound argument, or acknowledging that rationality is superior in making a fair judgment, implies that they must never feel another emotion. That type of thinking would be an example of

- **Jumping to extreme conclusions/actions,**
- **Mind reading,**

- **Drawing conclusions based on facts that could have other interpretations, and**
- **Assuming that the opposite party means something they may not mean.**

If it weren't for emotions, we could not enjoy art, children, or a lover. In fact, the idea of enjoying anything is emotional! I suggest that we invest in rational decision-making so that we can feel positive emotions about the result, knowing we have rationally balanced our emotional pleasure with a sense of ethics (see my book *Your Ethics are Immoral*) that functions in the real world.

Sometimes emotions help us make a decision when rationality has left us with information but no obvious preference. Have you ever weighed the pros and cons of a decision and then decided to leave it to chance by flipping a coin? Once flipped, however, you may find yourself resisting the result. That tells you that you feel more strongly about the opposite choice than you thought you did. Have you even written down the advantages of buying a car, let's say the rechargeable electric mini-coup, knowing it will save you $1000 a year in fuel costs, but goshdarnit, it just does not *feel* right, so you buy the 6-cylinder, gasoline-powered, sexy sportster, feeling that it fits your personality better. Choices like these have an important emotional element, which if ignored, will make you unhappy with your purchase overall, even if you are doing what is rationally best for yourself in one area.

I advocate factoring an emotional element into your decision so long as you will not hate yourself in the long run, and so long as you are willing to trade the practicality you lost for the positive emotional impact you gained. A friend of mine, having lost a dog that was her constant companion for twelve years, was both distressed at the loss and happy to have eliminated the burden of caring for the ailing pet. She finally would be free of the constant expenses of the veterinarian and the pet's medicines, and she would be free to date and travel again. Passing by a pet store, a girlfriend of hers encouraged her to buy a new little dog. My friend resisted, but her girlfriend insisted. She promised to help take care of the dog, said that it would be a great companion, etc. My friend bought the dog, discovered it was ill, and found herself back in the situation of caring for a sick dog. She kicked herself every day for having given in to her feelings of the moment without considering how she might feel in the long run. And the friend that goaded her emotions was not there to help.

There is also a connection between rationality and emotion. If we understand and rationally defend our values (those things that we wish to hold on to), we feel emotional about them. Of course, most people are emotional about that which they value, but they have never rationally figured out why those values are or should be important to them.

Ayn Rand wrote, "Emotions are not tools of cognition." It's not that your feelings are unimportant, but that they do not substitute for the logical consideration of empirical data. Those for whom "cognition" has a broader definition have contested her statement. If you consider cognition to be only *perception*, then emotion is part of the cognitive toolkit; however, if you consider cognition to be *understanding* or an attempt at *a reality-based assessment,* than rationality, not emotionality, is the appropriate tool.

Culturally, we have an abundance of excellent sources that can play on our emotions in ways that are acceptable and even desirable. When Simon Cowell hits the golden buzzer for the 10-year-old singer, I feel emotional every single time. Although I cannot sing well, the singer's success taps in me the idea of a goal that was set, worked for, and achieved. Therefore, I feel the associated emotion of earned gratification and know what value is at its core.

Every TV show, movie, novel, comic book, popular song, or piece of art is meant to effect our emotions. We watch, read, or listen to them because we *want* our emotions to be affected. Note how many political causes have been put into songs, novels, or films. Identifying with the characters in those arts allows us to bypass any careful thinking in favor of a gut reaction. Once again, there is nothing wrong with that *per se*, however, we should also have at the ready the rational faculties that we have (allegedly) developed in academia.

We want a balance so that our sympathies and idealism does not obfuscate the truth. If a "bum" is walking upright on the streets, asking for a dollar, you might say to yourself, "There are plenty of entry level jobs available today—this person should get one!" However, if an emaciated "homeless person" is asking for dollar, squatting near a cardboard crate that you assume to be his residence, you feel that you can easily spare the money since he should not have to live like that. Our emotions, serving as a short cut to a judgment that we may have previously arrived at rationally, help us make an instant decision. We do not know enough to determine whether one or the others of the street dwellers deserves our money, so we go with our gut, and we feel good about it. Unfortunately, sometimes we have been played because we did not have time or the ability to temper our emotions with facts.

When I moved out of my condominium apartment and into my new condominium townhouse, I had the opportunity to earn some additional income by renting the apartment. I paid a rental agency to evaluate potential lessees. It came up with a young couple, Sam and Sally, not married, but with a child from the woman's previous marriage. She was not working so I asked Sam for his tax returns to make sure they could afford the rent. This was something the agency should have done, but they had not. Sam did not proffer any 1040s, but instead introduced me to his boss who vouched for him and his work ethic. As a novice landlord and one who knew what it was like to have a minimum income, I decided that with two recommendations (his employer and the agency), the couple was acceptable. Her name was on the lease.

A good friend of mine had also set a positive standard for me by being an understanding and kind property owner who, once his renters were settled in, never raised their rent, even when market rates increased. He reasoned that once he found good tenants, he wanted them to stay, so he would treat them as well as he would treat employees. I agreed, of course, but unlike him, I had no track record with renters since this was my first renter's rodeo. Tenants traditionally consider landlords hardheaded and unemotional, and I certainly did not want to be one of those!

Within a few months, Sally had called me about the refrigerator in the apartment and I drove there to decide if it needed to be repaired or replaced. The refrigerator was frosted over from the freezer compartment into the lower compartment so one could barely close the door. I was shocked that she had not called me earlier, but even more shocked at the number of people in the apartment. There were two additional women in the living room and seven young children that were playing with finger paints on the carpet and walls without their mothers (or their caretakers, if they were not their mothers) controlling the mess. I wondered if Sally just did not care about other people's property, or if she assumed, as many had, that a landlord would not be considerate of her needs, so she was not about to be considerate of his property. I ordered a new refrigerator and it was installed by the end of the week.

A few months later, Sally stopped paying rent and the boyfriend was nowhere in sight. I let it go for one month and then told her that I would have to take her to court if she did not pay up. Unfortunately, court is exactly what happened. Of course, it was an instant judgment in my favor. Outside the courtroom, a man who described himself as Sally's friend handed me a check to cover the back rent. Great, I thought, maybe this guy will move in with her, even though his name is not on the lease, and things will get back to semi-normal. No, he did not move in, but in just a month or two, she moved out, leaving me with a messy apartment that had to be re-carpeted, repainted, and re-rented.

As an inexperienced landlord who wanted to be sensitive to a renter's situation, I had not taken the precautions that more practiced property owners would have taken. I had relied on my emotions in a situation that called for stricter and more realistic judgment. I noted that I had felt concern for her, but she had not felt concern for me: I still had to pay the mortgage and taxes on the property she had been renting, I still had to repair and refurbish the apartment so that it was rentable, and I still had to pay an agency to rent it. I certainly was not wealthy, but because she had less than I financially, she felt free to live at my expense. Because I had let my emotions rule, I had allowed her to do so.

Perhaps this was an exceptional incident. It would be unfair to judge all tenants by the actions of one. I had certainly been a great tenant at one time, my girlfriend had been a great tenant, and my landlord friend had rented to several great tenants. So, lesson learned—or so I thought—I rented the apartment again to Mr. Short, a single guy who worked for a computer company. Tax returns in order, he paid his rent on time…until he was laid off. Once again, I said he'd have to make good on two months back rent or I would have to take him to court. His girlfriend called me up telling me how heartless I was as a rich property owner. I don't know if she expected me to allow him free rent, and if so, on what grounds, but she certainly wanted something from me, rather than her finding him a job that may have been below his technical skills but not below his ability to earn a paycheck. Her feelings about him were not going to pay his rent and my feelings about his losing his job were not going to pay my mortgage or property taxes. It was not a time for feelings but for simple facts: no rent, no occupancy. "Judge," Mr. Short said in court, "I have had a nasty bout of unemployment."

The judge said, "Mr. Short, did you sign this lease?"

"Yes, sir."

"Then you owe two months' back rent. Decided in favor of the plaintiff."

But winning the case is not the same as being paid. The rent was not only never delivered, but in accordance with Massachusetts law, I had to pay for moving him out and storing his belongings until he could find another apartment—something he could not do without a job.

I had been less softhearted in this case, but I still had evidently not learned my lesson. Instead, I felt it must have been my choice of the specific lessee that had created my bad luck. I would be more careful in renting out my parents' old house—the one where I had spent my youth. Only qual-ity clientele for me! Two friends of mine, Mike and Mary, with a young child, were nearing the end of their lease and fell in love with the east side of my parents' duplex. I had been renting it to a very nice woman who was living with her boyfriend, but they had moved out, illegally subletting it to acquaintances. Having asked all tenants and pseudo-tenants to clear out within a month, I was ready to repair, re-paint, and re-carpet the place. "No," Mike and Mary begged. "Let us move in right away. We don't care about the carpet or paint."

Long story short: although they moved in at a monthly rent much lower than the apartment was worth on the market, they still saw fit to call the town (not me, mind you, but the town) to complain about a crack in a window and lead paint on the walls (something about which I was completely unaware). $50,000 of my savings spent, the apartment was de-leaded, they moved out, and I sold the house, disgusted that friends would treat me as an opponent simply because I had been a landlord. Moral? Probably that no good deed goes unpunished. I had finally learned my lesson: I could afford to decide by emotion only if I were willing to bear the cost of someone taking advantage of that decision.

When people appeal to your emotions, often they have no intention of compensating you for cutting them slack, giving them a break, or doing them a favor. They are being self-interested while appealing to you *not* to be self-interested.

In a wider realm like politics, people are free to make decisions based on emotions, of course, but those who wish to convince others to vote for a policy that follows their emotional instincts rather than one based on the available facts, *are taking no risks at all*. They are simply appealing to others to *feel* they way *they* feel. At whose expense?

There are emotionally "attuned" people who believe they understand a situation in their hearts (i.e. emotionally). On February 1, 2006, Bill O'Reilly (more or less on the Right and definitely a traditionalist) interviewed Whoopi Goldberg (definitely on the Left and more or less a non-traditionalist) concerning The War in Iraq. Whoopi said, "When I take a stance on something, all I can talk to you about is how I feel about it and why. And I don't have to justify it, and you don't have to listen to it. But it is impor-tant for everyone to know that they have an opinion and they have a — have a right to express it." She was saying that it is allowable to have an opinion based on feelings. After all, people don't have to listen to it. Of course, technically, this is correct. She was also saying that it was unnecessary to justify her feelings. Also true.

Bill responded with, "But your opinion is a little bit more heard than somebody — than 'Sally' in Charlotte…."

GOLDBERG: "No different than yours."

O'REILLY: "No, but I back mine up all day long with facts and everything else."

GOLDBERG: "But you know what? Your opinion is your opinion. And if you want to go…"

O'REILLY: "Based on facts."

GOLDBERG: "And if you want to go and get lots of facts and not go from your heart…. I go from my heart."

Whoopi seemed to believe that it was appropriate to have the opinion first and then find the facts to back it up, but only if you wanted to. This may be the natural way opinions are solidified, but often it is the opinions, rather than the facts, that remain immutable without justification. People look for selective facts to back up what their gut tells them and ignore facts that disprove their feelings. That's called Confirmation Bias. Whoopi also seemed to believe that since one was free to have an opinion, and free to express that opinion, that one's opinion was as valid/valuable/acceptable as any other. That is to say, that the third party, the audience, should react to the opinion itself rather than the reasons why the opinion was formed. How could she justify her opinions without facts? Without an objective analysis, wouldn't those opinions have to be emotional and subjective? Yet she did not recognize any value to O'Reilly's attempt at empirical evidence leading toward an attempt at objective justification.

Ironically (and this was true during most of their interchanges on *The O'Reilly Factor* program), she remained *calmer and less animated than he*. A second irony is that in a famous discussion with O'Reilly regarding the 9/11 attack that occurred on her program *The View*, while Bill was as animated as usual, Whoopi became *incensed enough* to walk off the set.

Certainly, important ideas can make us passionate. Does that mean we should judge what each of these commentators stood for based on their level of passion?

REALITY SHOULD BE THE REFEREE

I do not have a background in psychology, but I would hazard a guess that there are people who find it difficult, simply due to a genetic predisposition, to avoid shading their thinking with a heavy dose of emotionality. I have been in several "discussions" in which not only did opponents ignore the facts, but also doubled down with another layer of emotion rather than respond to my reasoning. Frankly,

I hope I am wrong about emotionality being determined largely by DNA, but I believe it is a possibility. As with most nature/nurture arguments, there are probably shades of variation in the middle. If so, the people in that middle ground are a possible audience to which a rational argument can appeal.

Although one party might win over an audience more easily than another, ultimately objective reality itself should be the referee, judge, and jury of any idea, proposal, or plan. Where an opinion is subjective, putting that opinion into action makes it objective—it occurs in the real world. Unfortunately, even though we have records in writing, audio, and video of past points-of-view to inform us of their accuracy in the real world, we seem able to ignore that empirical evidence in favor of yet another position that seems emotionally satisfying.

Whenever a position has not turned out as predicted, its supporters are prepared with one explanation after another:
(1) the negative result was a unique occurrence that does not reflect the wider reality,
(2) the results were not accurately compiled/calculated,
(3) the tested plan was not the plan as originally proposed,
(4) the situation in which the plan was tested was not the situation for which the plan was originally intended,

(5) the position was devised years ago; the situation has changed now,
(6) the position was generally correct, but it looks incorrect because real-time adjustments were not added during its execution,
(7) the plan may have failed then, but now we have learned much more about how to make it work,
(8) although the plan did not work as well as initially projected, it actually worked better than the opponent's plan would have worked, etc.

Ironically, each of these "explanations" depends on some subjective factor influencing the test. In other words, the excuses suggest that we cannot trust a real world test as an objective test because objectivity never exists. Tests are always colored by someone's subjectivity. This is a corollary of the Postmodernist thinking that has been increasingly favored in American colleges since the 1960s. But if there can be no objective test, how would we know if their ideas were to go right? If all real world tests are subject to repudiation because of invading subjectivity, why employ tests at all? How can anyone's point-of-view be proven more accurate than anyone else's?

I suggested in Chapter 8 that a convincing tactic, in the face of misleading accusations and claims, is to suggest that opponents mutually design a test that both will accept. This tactic works well when an emotional opponent

is sincerely seeking the truth, not so well when adherence
to ideology is more important to an opponent than truth.
Seldom do ideologues consent have their claims tested,
either because they do not trust the objectivity of the test, or
because they do not want to be proven incorrect. Their way
should be correct, after all, so the real world is less important
than their attractive ideal.

How do we normally avoid being taken in by everyday scams? Why don't we believe that a Nigerian Prince
really intends to leave a fortune in diamonds to the first person that answers his email? Isn't it because the vision seems
unrealistic? But what if the visions seemed feasible and the
promised ideals were eminently desirable? Isn't that why
a certain percentage of people are financially duped every
year? Political plans can be financial scams as well, or they
can be sincere and nevertheless end with the same conse-
quence that a scam would produce.

The average person recognizes that positions put
into practice will have consequences. In accepting that truth,
a person would tend to defer to whatever reality teaches. But
it doesn't always happen this way. An average person becomes a momentary Pollyanna when an emotional argument
promises a benefit that is enticing enough (whether or not

that benefit can be delivered) to suspend his disbelief. Since the promised benefit is so desirable, the person may want it to work and thus will defend it's application, despite its negative record. This is a sort of projected confirmation bias.

If it can be shown in good faith and in a real world test that the proposed position or program does not bring about the ideal, it would be reasonable to assume that most people would shed the idealism and reject the proposed position, right? But wait! There is a problem. The average person, besieged with both excuses and new ideals, will often readjust his/her preferences to favor the new ideals. Why? I suspect that he/she sincerely wants to improve the real world by aiming for the ideal world. That is not a problem in itself. The problem is expecting that the ideal will occur in the real world *just because it is a more desirable vision*. But, reality does not conform to visions; visions must conform to reality.

If ideals are supported only by emotions ("We want this to be true!"), they have a very small chance of successfully interfacing with reality. A simple example is The Peace Movement of the 1960s. No one can argue that peace is generally more desirable than war, but simply wanting the planet to be peaceful is an idealistic position that, in the real world, turns into fantasy. Wanting peace unilaterally does not make it come to fruition multilaterally. Simply desiring peace, simply acting without animosity, simply holding peace demonstrations, gatherings, and prayer groups cannot account for those who would gladly take advantage of well-meaning pacifists. And wanting peace so badly that you would advocate that your government unilaterally disarm, for example, is a formula for tragedy.

ALL YOU CAN DO IS THE BEST YOU CAN DO

I recently watched an educational video program on the history of the CIA. I understood the desirability, after World War II, for a U.S. government agency that could keep an eye on whatever enemy nations may have been planning. If they were spying on us, it only made sense to spy on them. This was the "fight fire with fire" approach, albeit the fire was cold. During a cold war, we needed to acquire advance knowledge of enemy plans, just as in a hot war. There were times, however, where the CIA justified to itself that not just spying, but also interfering with the politics of sovereign nations was acceptable—at first because our enemies did it, then because our enemies *would* do it, and then because we needed to do it to *prevent* our enemies from doing it. No one could devise a "fight fire with water" strategy except via the "water" of political negotiations. But negotiations often turned out to be shams or delaying tactics in the foreground while in the background secret agencies were attempting real-world interference.

As a result, I concluded that I did not support much of the CIA's covert actions, but neither did I trust other governments to refrain from nefarious sub-rosa activities. In international politics, there is no third party audience to which to appeal—no voting body that could change the disreputable actions of sovereign countries. The United Nations is the logical candidate to be that body, but they have never been willing, able, or objective enough to referee fairly the covert actions of nations. For the USA to be ethical and still be aware of its self-protection, all it could hope to do would be to make its fire as cool as possible—an act of temperature regulation that would differ from situation to situation and from administration to administration. There could be no permanent thermostat setting. If the USA let the CIA do what it felt necessary regardless of the sovereignty of other countries, other countries would do the same to the USA. If the USA eliminated or severely weakened the CIA, other countries would take advantage of that weakness. Ideally, the USA could restrict the CIA to information gathering and eliminate its covert operations—thus fighting fire with a much cooler kind of fire, but even that position might be insufficient to protect the USA in a world in which certain powers do not play fair.

We are left with simply doing the best we can do, as ethically as we can do it. I find that fact very unsatisfying, but I see no way around it. It may also be true of dealing with pre-feminist guerrilla argumentation. Tolerant passivity in the face of this type of argumentation is often non-functional, but using similar emotional tactics may simply extend the use of the very tactics we deplore. (NB: I explore another side of this point of view in Chapter 15, *The Frustration of Inspiration*.)

JUST DON'T

Non-engagement is the ultimate passivity, but it is not necessarily tolerant.

In *The Sacrifice of Shangrilla*, the third novel of the *Shangrilla Artifacts* trilogy, three friends, one of which is the Prince of Shangrilla, having grown up in a completely pacifist city-state, have been captured and forced to fight various opponents from other city-states. Because of their athletic training, they manage to win without harming their opponents. However, in a much-publicized event, all three are to compete in a non-violent athletic game, the winner of which will enter a death match with an unknown opponent. Each wishes to protect the other, so each wishes to win, but Prince Shang suggests another strategy: to play without scoring.

To deal with guerrilla argumentation, one can always simply avoid the argument. If a discussion unexpectedly turns into a disagreement in which one party uses guerrilla emotional tactics, one can simply say, "Okay," not in concession, but in acceptance of the situation, and refuse to engage any further.

Dropping out of contention can elicit a hostile reaction from a would-be opponent (to whose hostility you would act in a similarly disengaged fashion). But often after you overtly refuse to engage, if there is an audience, a few neutral people will approach you to hear what you really think. These are the people that are at least willing to listen to a rational argument, whether or not they decide to agree with you.

Dropping out strategically is another way of letting reality be the referee.

Chapter 12.

Moral Superiority and Ignorance

IS PETULANCE A RESULT OF ETHICAL COURAGE?

"Ethical courage" is simply being true to one's moral convictions. Having the courage to defend your ethics does not prove the validity of your ethical position although feeling ethical can carry with it a satisfaction and sense of superiority that is emotional. Have people adopted emotional arguments simply because they are sick and tired of others who "just don't get it [their moral superior position]"? Sure, but that assumes that the others just don't get it because they don't share the same ethics. Can a morally superior position be proven simply by emotional fervor? Some people think so and so they levy emotional arguments as if the value of their ethics is self-evident.

What about the fact-oriented person who becomes frustrated with the petulance of the emotional person? Dealing with petulance can make a person petulant, especially if the opposing person proffers pre-feminist argumentation while assuming moral superiority. The more frustrated one becomes, the touchier one gets. Even the most rational of people can become frustrated and touchy when his/her well-researched, well-implemented arguments fall on deaf ears. If you think you are being eminently rational and your arguments are still ignored by those who are not, avoid a bout of petulance by either employing counter-tactics or deciding to disengage.

Remember the last item on our guerrilla argumentation list?

- **Since I know I am virtuous, you cannot be.**

Why is name-calling the last tactic of those who use emotional guerrilla argumentation? Labeling is an emotional shortcut. When the guerrilla labels an opponent, in essence he/she truncates the argument by summarizing how the audience *should* feel. If the guerrilla can convince others that the opponent truly lives up to the label, e.g. is a racist, sexist, etc., no one would want to give that person a moment of attention. Voila! The guerrilla wins by labeling to elicit an emotion, not by leveling a convincing argument.

I remember personal disagreements in my youth when my sense of what I was *free* to do conflicted with an opponent's sense of what I *should* do, both "for my own good" and to be accepted by others. My very traditional, religious opponents would conclude with something like, "You are going to burn in Hell!" I hear these same sort of conclusions today, except they are coming from allegedly non-traditional people who do not use Hell for a threat, but nevertheless damn their opponents to the mundane mini-hells of Racism, Sexism, Homophobia, Islamophobia, Transgenderphobia, etc. In each case, the name caller assumes moral superiority. In each case, they become petulant when they cannot convince others with verbally adroit arguments preset by the "authorities" on their sides. They accepted those authorities (embodied in religions, political parties, or public figures) partially because those groups most clearly enunciated how they felt, but also because once the authority was accepted, they no longer had to sort through both sides of an argument. Once the label is launched, no further thinking is necessary. They sacrifice their independent thinking for belonging to like-minded pseudo-thinkers.

I do not mean to suggest that no movement or group or individual embodies what I think. In fact there are several. But I seldom join their causes or financially support them, nor do I stop evaluating what they say or do. Many times, I agree with 80% or 90% of what I hear from a speaker, for example, and feel that hers is the best available position for me to take. But that does not mean that tomorrow she will speak for me, or that I will align with her on other subjects.

IGNORANCE, GOVERNANCE, ECONOMICS, AND ETHICS

We align with causes, parties, churches, and personalities because they express our feelings in words and/or because they know more about the subject in question that we do. That is not unusual—the average Jane or Joe cannot possibly have a deep knowledge about specific subjects such as governance, theology, sociology, psychology, or economics. I would suggest, however, that Mr. Ecson deMobile's knowing a great deal about searching for and extracting crude oil from far off terrains does not mean he knows how the international market for oil arrives at per barrel prices or how the Saudi oil cartel operates. Ms. Belle Wetter may know a lot about how greenhouse gases might effect global warming, but she knows little about how contradictory factors effect global cooling or which countries have ignored the greenhouse guidelines they claim to support. Specialized expertise is not equivalent to generalized expertise, even within a similar field. When "experts" use their specialized knowledge to predict a generalized outcome, they assume no one else's specialized knowledge is relevant. Having mentally dismissed other points of view, they portray their vision as critical to the wellbeing of everyone around them. Otherwise, who would pay attention to them? Their vast knowledge in a limited area seems much more well-informed than the average person's limited knowledge in that specific area, so a few facts and a great deal of fervor can win over a relatively uninformed audience, especially if the fervor is imbued with a sense of morality.

Average people are confident about what is ultimately right and wrong, and often they feel strongly about it. But have they thought deeply about it? Have they thought about how to get to that ultimate right and avoid the wrongs on the way? They have a set of ethics, but do they know why they have adopted a set of ethics? Do they know how to ethically defend those ethics? Do they know the ethical repercussions of putting their ethics into practice?

It is much easier to manipulate people's feelings than to influence a careful thinker. Where feelings seem to come automatically, careful thinking is sometimes onerous. In a conversation with a friend of mine, during another automobile trip, she contended that emotions simply happen to a person while I contended that they were a result of values that, in turn, were a result of both personal experiences and a deeper understanding of how things work. Obviously, my contention was harder to explain and, if correct, more complicated to live with.

Why bother going to all that effort analyzing thoughts when your gut reaction will tell you the truth? The simple answer is because someone can manipulate your feelings more easily than your careful reasoning, therefore what you *feel* is true may not be. It doesn't mean you should abandon gut reactions, but it suggests that you should review and analyze your gut reactions during times when your gut does not need to react.

There is a parallel in martial arts training: martial artists train artificially and consciously to develop skills and reactions that can be called on instantly in a situation where there is no time for artificial or conscious reactions. In training a martial arts defense, one first recognizes the kind of attack, considers the kind of receptions, and then practices various kinds of reactions. At first, practice is slow, then increasingly quick. At first, practice is prearranged, then increasingly impromptu. In order to oppose a carefully constructed emotional argument, one must first recognize the kind of tactic being used, know about the subject at hand, and then formulate a rational counterargument, first carefully and slowly, then more extemporaneously. Very few people, regardless of education or position, are facile at this.

It is understandable that an audience would not be familiar with various kinds of argumentation, would not know very much about a given subject, and would not be able to fashion a counterpoint to an emotional tactic when their prime "expertise" is only the ethical positions they feel strongly about. The average audience, in my opinion, mentally converts its ethics to emotions and thus is ripe to be irrationally influenced. This does not mean that all emotional arguments are wrong, of course, only that, right or wrong, they can easily influence an audience of average people. Note that in today's world, that which passes as an argument is a clever phrase, marching poster, or meme. "Bumper sticker logic" bypasses the rational faculty and shoots directly for the emotional faculty.

Everyone is familiar with the concept of *caveat emptor* or "let the buyer beware". Growing up in a free market society in which there is a lot of choice, there are bound to be items and services for sale that are not quite what they claim to be. Sometimes this is done with intentional illegal deception, but more often it is done through legal but nonetheless misleading advertising that emphasizes virtues and ignores drawbacks. Most potential customers understand that advertising claims can be one-sided, exaggerated, or worded to entice. I recall a 7th grade class in which Mr. Hodges explained this to us, offered us examples, and then had us offer examples. I would suggest that thousands of Mr. Hodgeses do the same in todays' world. Further, I would suggest that they extend that explanation, without judgment or political commentary, to an explication of how logic and clear thinking works. Non-contradictory, non-deceptive thinking has been studied since the ancient Greeks, but somehow in recent decades has been absent from academia at every level.

THEIR REALITY VS. OUR REALITY

Why do even scholars ignore logical investigation in favor of fanciful but apparently new ideas they believe they can verbally justify without empirical data? It is easier to advance new ideas if they are rather free flowing and not subject to strict fact checking, debate, or testing. If a scholar wants to be published in an academic journal, he is likely to undergo some sort of peer review—strict research and logical argumentation will be necessary; however, if a scholar wants to publish his opinion in a national magazine, editors who know next-to-nothing about his subject will consider it for publication, just so they can have a "scholar" contribute to their magazine and enhance its saleability.

Many scholars in their realm and many politicians in their realm desire to be heard. The products of academics are ideas, and especially ideas that can be put into use. If their ideas convince politicians, those ideas have a better chance of entering into public policy or at least public notoriety, thus increasing book sales and the scholar's celebrity. "Great!" you may say, "What could be better than to have policies based on the ideas of brilliant minds?" Sounds good in theory, right? Please return to the previous section and read it again. Ideas *per se* are not necessarily functional. Only functional ideas are functional. Innovation *per se* is not necessarily helpful. Only helpful innovation is helpful. Ideas can come from experts without the ideas themselves being "expert" (i.e., proficient) at addressing a problem. In addition to which, the politicians who depend on scholarly ideas are not necessarily proficient judges of those ideas.

Many scholars desire to become noted "intellectuals". To maintain the "intellectual" status, academics have to come up with new interpretations of old ideas, since wholly new ideas are at a premium. However, if their ideas do not function as predicted in *our* reality, if they do not have successful results when subjected to real world testing, then the hypothetical "reality" of those academics and politicians is useless to us non-intellectual, non-experts living in what we thoughtlessly deem "the real world".

I knew a woman who loved idealistic thinking so much that she never allowed negative thoughts to enter "her reality". Unfortunately, this meant that she seldom allowed objective reality to enter her subjective reality. When faced with a severe winter storm after which ice blocked her doorway, she waxed about the lovely light-refracting qualities of the 6-foot icicles rather than clear a path to the street so that she could escape if necessary or so that others could safely enter to help her. There is nothing wrong with *enjoying* an icy challenge, but *ignoring* the need to face such a challenge can be self-destructive. And waiting for someone else to face it for you is freeloading, to say the least.

It is admittedly difficult for some people to give up ideals in favor of a less-than-perfect reality. In business, there is a saying that "the excellent is the enemy of the good", i.e. that if you wait until a product is perfect before sending it to market, you will never send it to market. How many products offer new-and-improved versions at regular intervals because obviously the original version was good, but not as good as it could have been, and certainly not perfect? Cynics might criticize that companies *plan* to have consumers constantly upgrade, thus extending their profit opportunities. This is called "planned obsolescence". But in our current fast-paced and competitive environment, if you don't release the best possible product as quickly as possible, some other company will. Thus, most businesses rush to market with a good product and make updating it relatively cheap and easy. It is true that if they have a dominant market share and a product that clients cannot do without, they might think more about maximizing their incomes with the current version of their product and less about rushing to market with new innovations. However, if they are too complacent, too locked in on their current success, another business will undercut their prices, improve the product, or find a completely new way to address the problem that the product initially solved.

Most businesses create a healthy balance between a good, functional product that serves their clients (albeit subject to improvement) and a marketing program that helps earn them profits, thus allowing them to further innovate and further serve their clientele with an improved product.

Imagine if people that find fault with the functional because it is not flawless compelled us to wait for perfection.

If "their reality" were one of ideals, when would they ever be satisfied? Those who use emotional guerrilla argumentation are seldom satisfied with a solution that is not ideal. Their feelings always reach out to the exceptions—those whose situation is not improved by a good (but not perfect) solution. That means their feelings will always have someone to whom to reach out. They will always be able to use an emotional argument fueled by someone who is not completely served, saved, or made whole by a pitiful 98.6% solution. They can always say, "What about the families that fall through the cracks?" or "What about the guy who can't afford to travel to the jobs you provide," or "What about the way people treat the undocumented immigrants from Southern Escondida who, through no fault of their own, have leprosy?" This is one of the reasons emotional arguments can be dangerous. If our hearts reach out to illegal immigrants from Southern Escondida with leprosy, we may not be able to reasonably take care of legal citizens with cancer. Since emotional choices are hard to make, people dominated by emotions want a situation in which no one will have to choose between those options. They want a Brave New World in which everybody is helped all the time and everybody is happy all the time. How this is to come about and at whose expense is a matter for the rational mind, so they simply ignore it.

In the realm of male/female relationships, an "idealistic" pre-feminist guerrilla tactic might be expressed in something like the following: "You never care about me. The kids have been wild today and you were not here so I had no backup. They made a holy mess in the living room and I had to clean it up—twice. You always miss my parents' anniversary as if they don't matter to you. They were so generous to give us that great wedding and you are so ungrateful. And another thing: You always leave it to me to feed the dog. You never do! Do you think I exist just to do what you are too inconsiderate to do? You don't even care about the dog!"

"But honey, I missed your parents anniversary only once, two years ago, and I am at work when the kids come home from school and when you feed the dog. So tell me, what is really bothering you?"

"Oh, you don't care!"

"I think I would if you'll tell me. Maybe I can take some burden off you. It would help if you could make a list and show me which things I could help with."

"See? That's just another thing I'll have to do!"

"Okay. Let's make the list together. You say what comes to mind and I'll write it down."

Note that, in the above encounter, if the husband is successful in both making his wife feel good again and helping her deal with real problems, he ignores her *ad hominem* arguments (see the next section below on CHARACTER ASSASSINATION), does *not try to create the ideal* situation, but finds a way for them to *work together* (see the section below on MORAL COLLABORATION). He gradually changes her reality to a more objective reality.

ARGUMENTATION INTO
CHARACTER ASSASSINATION

Why does the pre-feminist type of argumentation often end in labeling, a.k.a. name-calling? Perhaps it is because labeling is a blatant attempt at character assassination. Okay, but why does an attempt a character assassination link back to emotional argumentation?

Let's assume two men get into a squabble. They are not naturally given to rational argumentation any more than are women (even if they think they are). If they get emotional, they will start calling names just as the pre-feminist does. If they become too emotional, however, they will engage physically. Fighting is their last resort, but it can happen and, if it happens, it can be dangerous to both of them, especially if there was a developing enmity to being with. If two male "friends" get into a fight, they might end up saying that it was a good fight and go out for a drink afterwards. In everyday life, men who compete with men curtail their propensity to engage in a physical fight. The world has changed since the hunter-gatherer days. Gradually, through eons of social evolution, civilized people look at non-sportive combat as the mark of crudity and anti-intellectuality, neither of which are traditionally respected in everyday society. Men therefore have learned to sublimate their anger, especially in dealing with other men.

If two women get into a verbal match, they are less likely to come to blows, but if they do, they are less likely to make up. Instead, they may badmouth each other to their friends and to their opponent's friends, continuing the fight in the background by indirect means. One of these means is character assassination. Women who conflicted with women in pre-feminist times learned how to attain the upper hand without having to physically fight. Instead of fighting, they found a way to undercut or destroy the character of the rival who had offended them.

What about men competing with women? If there is a social stigma against anyone physically fighting, there is a double stigma against a man fighting a woman. But there is no stigma against a woman's using subtle character assassination. Men are therefore caught between a rock and a hard place if they choose to clash with women or if a woman chooses to clash with them. They cannot physically fight and they are not practiced at character assassination. But if men could master the art of pre-feminist character assassination, they would have weapons equal to pre-feminist women.

According to some psychologists, character assassination is a weapon favored by angry women, but both genders seem to employ it in today's political "discussions" and social media slugfests. The more direct "masculine" form of this disparagement is blatantly calling an opponent an adjectivally modified below-the-waist body part. Women are subtler but potentially more stinging about it. But wait! We are no longer in the pre-feminist era, are we? Today women act like men used to act, and men act like women used to act, thus we have both genders using both vulgar epithets as well as sardonic verbal cuts aimed at character assassination.

DEFLECTION VIA EXAGGERATED ADMISSION

Nothing accelerates one's jump into petulance like being verbally insulted. Returning the insult just exacerbates the situation. You can stay in the discussion by accepting the insult in a way that makes obvious your opponent's exaggerated labeling.

"You are nothing more than a mean-spirited racist!" says E. Z. McBate.

"Oh, I am so sorry!" you respond. "I have such a difficult time with that. If you say so, it must be true, so I'll have to work to improve myself."

PROTESTS, CIVIL DISOBEDIENCE, AND MORAL SUPERIORITY

Strikes, public demonstrations, and protests are accepted as among the time-honored traditions of a free American society, usually used after attempts at negotiation with authorities fail. Civil disobedience, made famous by Henry David Thoreau, is another one of those traditions, and in the mid-20th century it was used frequently during the Civil Rights Movement. Each is a way to show that you, and perhaps a number of kindred spirits, disagree with a law, a policy, or a behavior.

Demonstrations are intended not just to sway the opponent (usually a government or an owner), but are also meant to stimulate public awareness in an attempt to change either the buying or voting habits of enough people so that indirect pressure is put upon the company or government to change its ways. In essence, these methods are an attempt to assert ethical positions. Civil disobedience, even if employed by one person, says, "I am willing to endure the punishment assigned to my disobedience in order to make the public aware that my actions should not deserve such punishment."

Over the years, however, these actions have been intentionally altered. In some cases, those who have been civilly disobedient feel that they should *not* be punished for their actions, a position which undercuts the essence of the method. In other cases, demonstrations and protests become unruly and intentionally block traffic, destroy property, or even physically attack the people that allegedly represent "the other side". These actions are a contortion of civil disobedience that puts the suffering not on the disobedient actors, who seldom pay the penalty, but on the obedient innocents. My initial thought, and the thoughts of many others, is that once you intentionally change the nature of a protest so that it transgresses the rights of others, you have lost your argument. However, in recent years, another interpretation has risen: "I am willing to break the law and transgress the rights of others because my position is so morally superior." This is **"Since I know I am virtuous, you cannot be,"** on steroids. It is taking those steroids while expecting no side effects. In fact, not only will the transgressor expect to be relatively free of pain or punishment, but also he/she has transferred the pain and punishment to others, in essence saying, "I am so morally superior, I get to sacrifice others."

Note that the larger the demonstration and the more it gets out of hand, the less frequently rational discourse is attempted. An action that intentionally breaks laws is a way to consolidate emotion on one side and eliminate a reasoned review of the issues at hand. It is daring law enforcement to act and make the disobedient look like the victims. The perpetrators throw temper tantrums, wagering that mom and dad will not spank them or put them in time-out. Their incivility is not civil disobedience but an attempt at igniting a civil war.

It is, of course, always possible that those who engage in strikes, public demonstrations, protests, and civil disobedience, violent or non-violent, are morally correct. However, if people accept that destroying property and preventing the exercise of civil liberties is a legitimate way to make an argument, they are actually tolerating civil war in the guise of disagreement. They are not only saying "I am so obviously right that, you must be wrong," but also, "I am so obviously right that I am willing to start a war."

WHAT WAR IS

War is rationally planned destruction to justify and defend strongly held emotions about moral superiority. Whenever people use destructive tactics while hiding behind traditionally accepted practices, they are waging a guerrilla war.

Petulant argumentation tries to illicit strong emotions in lieu of a good faith discussion. It is not actual war, of course, but it assumes "Since I know I am virtuous, you cannot be", thus, it wishes to emerge victorious rather than discover either objective truth or common ground. What are the chances that people who use our list of guerrilla tactics will at least agree to disagree? Since they believe that they have morality on their side, they also believe that "if you are not part of the solution, you are part of the problem". In other words, "I am moral. Not only are my opponents immoral, but also those who have not made up their minds are immoral!" Seems like a stacked deck to me. It is the worst kind of absolutism.

Certainly, people are free to feel this way, but using that kind of "heads I win, tails you lose" argument is nothing more than sophisticated name-calling. To refer back to our list of tactics again, using "if you are not part of the solution, you are part of the problem" is **dwelling on what other side *doesn't* do, rather than evaluating what it does.** And it is an attempt to stifle any rational discussion or disagreement.

The most recent version of this is, "Silence = Compliance". (See Chapter 6, *Digital Thinking*). Phrases like these paint everything black or white without the possibility of speckles or shades of gray. They attempt to morally shame people to join "the good guys", without any attempt to investigate the situation. "If you don't support defunding the police, you are complying with police brutality." Huh? You mean to say there is no other way to prevent police brutality? Yours is the only possible moral position to take?

Imagine if Ms. Peza Urhardt said, "Thou Shalt Not Kill means that you should never defend yourself or your country." You don't want to kill, but you do want to defend your country. If you disagree, according to Ms. Urhardt, you are allegedly complicit with murderers. But if you agree, you are not only unpatriotic but also complicit in the destruction of the republic. You might respond with, "Wait! Give me more information! What if I were to accidentally cause the death of someone trying to blow up congress? What if we destroy a plague of locusts to save our crops? And, doesn't that mean we cannot eat meat anymore? Wait! Plants are alive, too! No killing plants, either?"

Ms. Urhardt counters by saying, "That's just a *reductio ad absurdum* argument. Thou shalt not kill. If you don't comply, you are a murderer. And, if you are silent about this you are compliant with murder."

"No," you explain, "Silence Equals Compliance is the *reductio ad absurdum* argument! It tries to reduce complicated conceptions into simplistic responses. It tries to ignore details in favor of absolutism." This is precisely what is done when one decides to go to war—one accepts absolutism and moral superiority.

I am not opposed to *temporary* absolutism. There are things that I feel are absolutely right and no one is likely to sway my opinion. However, if I am not at least open to hearing reasoned arguments on the other side, if I do not accept that *the evidence at hand* might modify my opinion at least a little, I should not be engaging in argumentation at all. Instead, I should disengage completely and/or prepare for a conflict that will not be decided rationally, but by force.

IMMORAL COMPROMISE VS. MORAL COLLABORATION

When Ms. Peza Urhardt assumes moral superiority, she eschews compromise because compromise to her would be immoral. However, your simply conceding victory to Ms. Urhardt does not make you moral. What if you have the morally superior position? Would you then wish to compromise just to keep the peace? In male/female relationships, compromising to keep the peace may be laudable in the short run since it values the relationship over winning in the moment, but in the long run, constant compromise breeds resentment.

In other kinds of relationships, constant compromise allows the opposite party to demand twice as much in expectation of receiving half of what they demand. We saw this kind of strategy when countries kept compromising with Hitler's claims to their lands. He did not go away satisfied, but instead kept encroaching. In the pre-feminist '50s, women compromised in order not to get into a conflict with their husbands. Feminists said that compromise meant that the husbands would just assume the woman would always give in and thus he would not try to meet her even half way. They recognized that incremental submission just to keep the peace is amoral at best and in some situations is immoral. It is akin to allowing rioters and looters to "blow off steam" so that police will not be hurt enforcing the law. Even if the riot cools off, rioters and looters will know that the next time they wish to break the law, they are less likely to be opposed. In the meantime the rioters win, everyone's respect for the police diminishes, and the business owners lose the most.

Do not confuse immoral compromise with moral compromise. Sometimes, in order to take any action forward, compromise has to be made. A rigidity that says, "I will never compromise" suggests the "my way or the highway" mentality, while an eagerness to compromise suggests, "since I have no moral backbone, I'll go your way."

You might argue, "But, if you do not compromise, the only thing left is war." Maybe; but maybe there are other strategies that can engage those people who feel they are morally superior, as long *as they hold similar fundamental ethical values, but use different ways to apply them.* I wrote *10 Common Values* to make obvious the everyday beliefs many political opponents have in common. Below, I'd like to suggest ways in which well-meaning political opponents could cooperate, collaborate, or at least come together for a time.

Mutually designed tests. I have already suggested proposing a mutually designed test to adjudicate the value of each person's position. If both sides can agree on an impartial judge, the very act of designing such a test will help harmonize the opponents. Even if you do not design the test together but agree upon what, in the real world, would constitute a valid test, then you can postpone the disagreement until the facts are in. If Party A, the rational argumentation side, is completely vindicated and Party B completely vanquished, it would be wise for Party A to throw a lifeline to Party B in the form of understanding how Party B could think the way he/she did. This increases the chances for harmony and helps people see that "the hard facts" side can be considerate, as well.

Working together to open the dialogue. If a test cannot be designed, the way to collaborate may be creating a more open forum. Instead of suggesting that your opponent locate the best debaters on his side, have him pick out the best debaters on *your* side for your approval. You, in turn, choose the best debaters on *his* side for his approval. Even if you can't get them all together for a panel discussion, you can mutually decide to read or listen to them, take notes, and get together to debate again.

Common enemy. During The Cold War, many people quipped that the only thing that could unify the East and the West would be an invasion from Mars. If we wait for an invasion from Mars, we are not likely to collaborate soon. Is there a common foe, even a theoretical or philosophical one, on which both sides can agree? In fact, people are so politicized now that even national challenges like a virus, record unemployment, another country interfering with our elections, or another country stealing our businesses' secrets is not enemy enough to create a common external focus. I therefore suggest choosing a *goal* that you and the opponent both support, then looking for a commonly agreed upon reason that goal has not been achieved. You may disagree with most of the reasons, but it is possible to find one facet of agreement and work together on that.

A PARTIAL WITHDRAWAL TO PREVENT A WAR

As mentioned earlier, there comes a time when emotional arguments do not relent and your rational arguments are labeled rather than debated. If there is no possibility of rational contest, compromise, or collaboration, first withdraw from any contention and watch how things develop from an outside vantage point. Sometimes they cool down by themselves. Sometimes the emotional side contradicts itself and loses adherents. Sometimes they find something else to be emotional about and the formerly contested issue is put aside. Unfortunately, when emotional arguments do not relent, one also has to prepare for a complete secession of discussion, debate, or negotiations.

Just as I have always hesitated to join a cause, I also have hesitated to jump into a conflict, except of course to quell it when possible. Decades ago, I was teaching a series of martial arts seminars in France. My host was incensed that a longtime friend from Belgium was not treating him or his seminar series the way he had come to expect. At a group dinner, he began to express his anger at his friend, who was absent, while his students either stayed silent or nodded in agreement. Of course, they would not be comfortable disagreeing with my host, especially not during a dinner that was meant to celebrate the seminar series itself. Knowing that if I interjected I had less to lose than his students, but also knowing that I probably did not understand the history of or the details of the alleged infraction, I did my best to calm my host by suggesting that if the offending party had been considered a friend for many years, there was a good chance that either he had a pressing reason for doing whatever he did or that there had been some miscommunication. There was no need to start hostilities without learning more, and no need to assume that a friend of long duration for no apparent reason suddenly had become an enemy. As a neutral party, I was suggesting a partial withdrawal to prevent a war. Luckily, I was invited back the following year because of "my knowledge, technique, fairness, and calm attitude."

Chapter 13.

Media or Medea?

The Medea of Greek myth was the daughter of King Aertes and a sorceress, who fell in love with Jason (of Argonaut fame) and helped him complete a number of "impossible" tasks that had been assigned by her father, before Aertes would surrender The Golden Fleece. Medea helped Jason complete tasks by using her special powers—powers Jason would not have had without her. In essence, Medea sided against her father and with her lover.

In contemporary times, when we refer to The Media, we mean the communication organizations—newspapers, magazines, TV news networks, Internet news sources, and social media. Their special power is informing people about current events so that people can make reasonable decisions on how to act, spend their money, and vote. Like the Medea of myth, the media seems to have fallen in love and taken sides, and in the process, created some myths of their own.

Although, at this writing, most of the TV media leans to the Left, there are a couple of outlets that lean Right. Although most of the radio media leans to the Right, a few lean Left. Although the sum total of media influence (as listed above plus Hollywood, high tech, search engines, etc.) seems to favor the Left (see Tim Grossclose's book *Left Turn*), that imbalance is not the problem, in my opinion. The problem is that none of the outlets seems to know the meaning of the word "objective". Every media outlet, with the exceptions of the few individual news shows that try to be neutral—every media outlet takes a side and "helps" those they favor by using the "sorcery" of their public presentation. In other words, what used to be news—information for the average citizen—is frequently propaganda.

Propaganda can be delivered in many ways: (1) by canceling all news items that do not support the favored narrative, (2) by using positive phrases to describe the favored narrative and negative phrases to describe the unapproved, (3) by dropping the relevant context of a story, (4) by using set up scenes or "crisis actors" to make the visual of a story seem more dramatic, (5) by claiming the inaccuracy of a conflicting story or falsely fact-checking it, etc. Some of these are delivered in a guerrilla fashion, but more frequently in today's world, little about them is furtive. In fact, instead of acting like the dominated pre-feminist woman who has to stand up for herself, they act like the overly dominant man who is shaking a fist at the sneaky (and allegedly inferior) guerrilla that dares to oppose him.

There are many tactics that news outlets use to slant their delivery, but for this discussion, I am concerned only with emotional argumentation.

TALKING HEADS AND HEADLINES

TV news offers viewers two types of shows: those that give opinions about the news and those that simply report the news.

A news commentary show that invites guests to discuss the host's opinion makes a direct appeal to the audience, often using emotional argumentation. The host's opinions are first delivered in a passionate monologue that is like the editorial page of the newspaper. The guests then add their support to the opinion. Occasionally, when a guest offers an opposite opinion, viewers can actually witness a debate unless, of course, that guest is outnumbered or otherwise not allowed to speak freely. In this kind of panel discussion, you will often see our list of guerrilla tactics employed.

The TV programs that simply report the news may be slanted, but they generally do not use argumentation because there is no debate opponent and because they want their deliveries to at least appear factual. Instead of emotional argumentation, they use the equivalent of biased headlines: actual on-screen graphics, Chyrons (superimposed sub-graphics) and crawls, or verbal teasers for the next segment. Headlines of newspapers have always served to give the essence of a story in case the reader would rather spend time reading other stories. That is why newspapers used to feature main headlines and then smaller subsequent headlines—so people not interested in the details could still get the general gist of the story. If the headline is misleading, however, the less-than-careful reader will accept the headline as truth and move on. The same holds true when a talking head offers a headline.

Headlines are also meant to draw the audience into a story, of course, so they will have an element of emotionality. But I have noticed that in the last few decades they increasingly appear more like advertisements promising you INSTANT RELIEF FROM ACID INDIGESTION, only to deliver partial relief and after 30+ minutes. Ironically, the headlines themselves sometimes deliver instant indigestion. I am not talking about the sometimes unintentionally silly headlines that papers print, like: HOMICIDE VICTIMS RARELY TALK TO POLICE, but those that were either intentionally misleading or misleading because no one cared to double check the headlines' implications. Some of these are relatively minor infractions, even if their subjects are important:

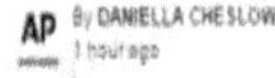

2 Palestinians killed following stabbing attack in Jerusalem

AP By DANIELLA CHESLOW
    1 hour ago

JERUSALEM (AP) — Two Palestinian assailants were shot and killed on Wednesday after stabbing Jewish pedestrians outside Jerusalem's Old City, Israeli police said, the latest in an unrelenting

As it turns out, an officer was also stabbed before the shooting.

U.S. Mistakenly Bombs Allies in Syria, Killing 18

In reality, a Kurdish-Arab coalition allied with the U.S. was killed after it provided the wrong coordinates for the bombs.

Some headlines are more egregious, like "accurate" headlines that communicate the wrong message such as: **NUMBER OF NATIONWIDE BURGLARIES GOING UP**. But, when you read the article, it suggests that the number is up by 1% over last year's all-time low. Or, how about: **PRESIDENT LOWERS DEFICIT BY 10%**. But, when you read the article, it explains that although the percentage of government expenditures this year was 10% less than the taxes collected, the amount of taxes this year increased by 20%, neither of which had much to do with the chief executive.

Some headlines give up the idea of accuracy in favor of keeping your interest. The following fictional headlines will, I believe, jog your memory of real "headlines" you have heard on TV.

"ALL HELL BROKE LOOSE WHEN NANCY

PELOSI WALKED ONTO THE HOUSE FLOOR WEDNESDAY…. Details after the break." After the commercials, we discover that someone delivered a fiery address that day, although it was unrelated to Ms. Pelosi walking onto the House floor.

"CORONA VIRUS CASES HIT AN ALL-TIME HIGH AND NO ONE SEEMS TO CARE…. We'll explain after the break." Then we discover that although cases hit an all-time high, that increase was predicted due to additional testing, and that virus deaths had hit an all-time low.

"SCHOOLS ARE FAILING AND YOU ARE PAYING FOR IT…. More after the break." Rather than the story being about schools producing students that cannot pass exams or graduate, we discover that some schools are actually failing to adhere to The Department of Education's guidelines because they dispute the one-size-fits-all governments rules.

"THIS MEANS…"

When you tune in to a news analysis or commentary program, you expect an opinion based on a news event. However, what you often receive is one person's opinion hidden behind a statement of alleged truth—subjective analysis portrayed as objective fact.

Let's assume that your favorite news analyst reports the following: "In an interview with NPR officials yesterday afternoon, former President Clinton said that National Public Radio is the only source of news he trusts when it comes to understanding The Jeffrey Epstein case." But the program's host then goes on to say: "This means that NPR has obviously whitewashed their coverage to downplay President Clinton's relationship with Epstein." Well, no Mr. Analyst, it does not *mean* that. Even if I were to agree with your conspiracy theory that NPR had been encouraged, pressured, or paid off to show Clinton in a positive light, the statement you quoted could simply mean that President Clinton trusts public radio reporting over commercial radio reporting. But you, Mr. Analyst, feel obliged to interpret Clinton's words for me, as if I were incapable of coming to my own conclusion. All you had to say was, "It seems to me…," or "In my opinion…," but you take the next step by coming to conclusions for me.

Even worse, in my opinion, are those talking heads that state their opinion as the truth, without even the qualification of "this means".

THE MEME MACHINE…

The egregiously poor reporting and slanted deliveries of the news are equaled by verbally and visually clever memes on social media. They act like headlines (and perhaps the first few lines of a news story) that have ingested emotional stimulants.

Here are a few misleading memes, followed by either the actual story or a less volatile interpretation of the graphic.

Meme Headline Fraud:

No, ICE agents were not opening a Dachau-like facility on American soil. In fact, they were disinfecting illegal alien detainees. The garish headline, repeated ten separate times, and the initial paragraphs that serve as the lead-in, are a full-blown attempt to make ICE agents appear like Nazis. Even if the disinfectant had been applied incorrectly or carelessly, the emotional headline was not emphasizing that, but was slanted to portray U.S. government agents as Hitleresque.

Conflating Terms to Incite:

Initially published on Facebook by a friend just as the protests regarding the killing of George Floyd were turning into riots and looting, I challenged the meme, saying that it should not conflate the protests shown in the lower section with the riots shown in the upper section, and said that I knew my friend would not want riots. The friend who posted the meme thought I did not get what she really meant. I felt that she did not get what she was really implying. In an attempt to clear it up, she posted the well-known 1951 Langston Hughes poem, as follows:

> What happens to a dream deferred?
> Does it dry up
> Like a raisin in the sun?
> Or fester like a sore--
> And then run?
> Does it stink like rotten meat?
> Or crust and sugar over--
> like a syrupy sweet?
> Maybe it just sags
> like a heavy load.
> Or does it explode?

Does this suggest that if Langston Hughes believes that a dream deferred can explode, then *ipso facto* riots are an *appropriate* substitute for protests? But even if we accept my friend's stated intention, the actual meme says that those who fashioned smaller, non-violent civil protests were told that they could not do so. But they *did* in fact fashion those smaller public protests. People that disagreed with their method of protest did not tell them they could not wear a t-shirt or could not kneel. If people *dislike* a method of protest, it is not the same as their preventing that method of protest. In fact, even if the protestors' employers ordered them not to use their sport, for example, as a venue for social protest, the news media carried their messages far and wide, anyway, so that their sentiments were not quashed at all. I'm sure my friend did not want to suggest that riots are a justifiable way to protest simply because people disagreed with an earlier kind of protest, but that's what the meme suggests, in my humble opinion.

The emotion behind not wanting to tolerate unwarranted police violence is so strong that many will see the meme and unconsciously accept the validity of rioting and looting even though they would not consciously condone them.

A Leap of Faith…er…Reason:

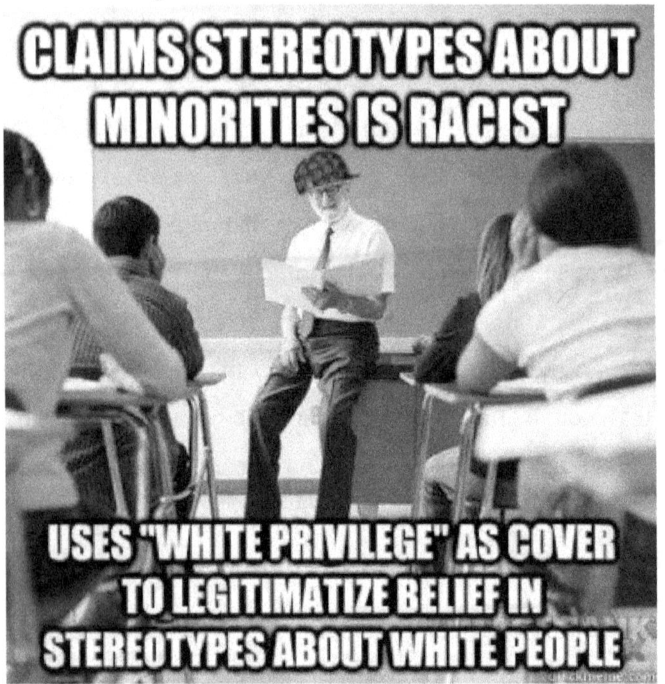

Certainly stereotypes about minorities can be racist, so the top line pulls us in. How about the second line? Who allegedly uses "white privilege"? Although it is not defined, one would have to assume it is the teacher in the picture. What is "white privilege"? Because it is undefined, you can fill in your own meaning. How is some definition of white privilege "covering" for an attempt to legitimize stereotypes about Whites? If stereotypes about white people were legitimized, that would also be racist, so I am assuming the meme is trying to suggest that pro-White beliefs, although racist, are okay with Whites—even those Whites who decry negative stereotypes about Blacks. Whew! That is a sincere attempt to take a lot for granted in order to beat a conclusion (if I am even correct about the conclusion) in to your brain!

First, we must assume that teachers are somehow trying to foist a stereotype. That's a bias we could call "teacher-ism": assuming all teachers have the same negative agenda by dint of their profession. Second, what stereotypes would white teachers want to legitimize? I would assume teachers would want to legitimize their intellectual authority in the classroom, but they have no need to (and there is no evidence that they try to) legitimize some sort of White agenda.

Repairing a comparison:

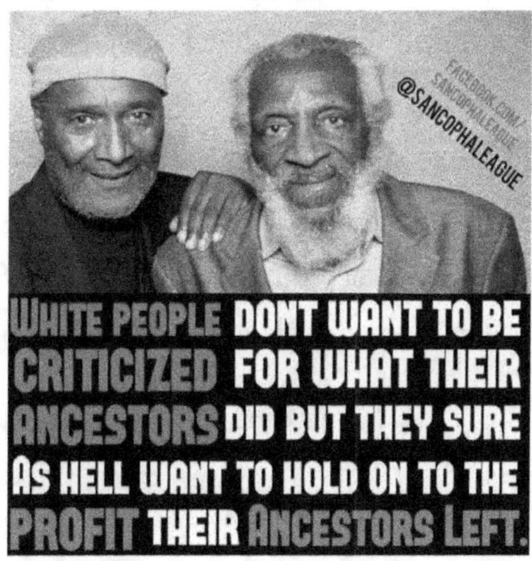

This exemplifies another kind of leap of faith. In logic, it is called A False Premise or Begging the Question. It is fascinating to me that this meme uses two true clauses to imply (at least in my opinion) a false conclusion. As regards the first part of the sentence: certainly it is true that "white people" do not want to be criticized for what their ancestors did. Neither would Asians or Blacks want to be criticized for what their ancestors did. To do so would mean you assume that guilt is in the bloodstream and is inherited. By that logic, if you cross the border illegally with Fentanyl in your possession, both you *and* your children's children should be imprisoned. Every human being, regardless of race, wants to hold on to as much of their inheritance (note the use of the word "profit") left by their ancestors as they can. Unless the creators of this meme support a 100% inheritance tax, no one is exempt from wanting to retain what their progenitors earned.

Again, one has to intuit (mind-read) what the meme means. Before I wrote down my assumptions about it, I visited the Facebook page noted in its upper corner. The first few posts I saw suggested that Black people should be armed for self-protection. Sounds fair. The reason given, however, was that Blacks are being abducted and lynched, a notion for which no evidence is presented. It would not be fair to type the league or its page because of a few posts, but several posts on that page helped me draw a conclusion based on rhetoric often used when pitting Blacks against White (even if the intention were simply to defend Blacks from Whites, as in the initial intention of The Black Panther Movement in the 1970s). My conclusion was that the above meme is suggesting that the wealth own by Whites occurred because of the sweat and tears of Blacks.

Assuming I am correct about what the meme intends to imply, let me offer a few comments to either repair the comparison or put it aside as another leap of faith. I balk at generalities that turn into stereotypes. It was definitely white people that owned black slaves for 100 years in the U.S. but there were many *more* white people that did not own slaves. "Oh, but they tolerated slave ownership!" you say. True, many did. Many more did not. That's one of the reasons the Civil War was fought. Several decades after the end of that war, immigrants from Europe entered the U.S. I am a grandson of two such families. They never owned slaves nor tolerated neighbors who owned slaves, but they are lumped into the collective of "white people".

If much of a slave state's economy was built on the back of slaves prior to the Civil War, those slaves could easily justify a demand for reparations from those slave owners.

Their descendants, however, cannot justifiably demand reparations from the descendants of slave owners, who never owned slaves, and certainly not from the descendants of immigrants from Europe. Guilt is not passed down through the blood of a relative let alone the skin tone of someone whom the guilty party never knew, and never even imagined knowing.

If this were not so, think of what other sort of guilt could be heaped upon any number of "collectives" whose ancestors were nasty. German, Italians, and Japanese would still be paying for their part in World War II. The Russian and Chinese governments would be compensating their own people for the millions of citizens their authoritarian governments put to death. The U.S. would have to pay Japan if not for those killed during the two nuclear blasts that ended the Second World War, then for the deaths due to the aftermath of the fallout. Africans would have to pay other Africans for their part in the slave trade. Almost everyone we know would be collectively related to some guilty party somewhere, so pay up! How dare you want to hold on the "profit" your ancestors left!

MY SORT OF MEME

I never publish anything political on my Facebook page. In fact, I rarely publish any meme on my Facebook page, but when I do, I try to emphasize a philosophical principle that I support, and that other people probably support, but have not been fully cognizant of. Here are my three favorites:

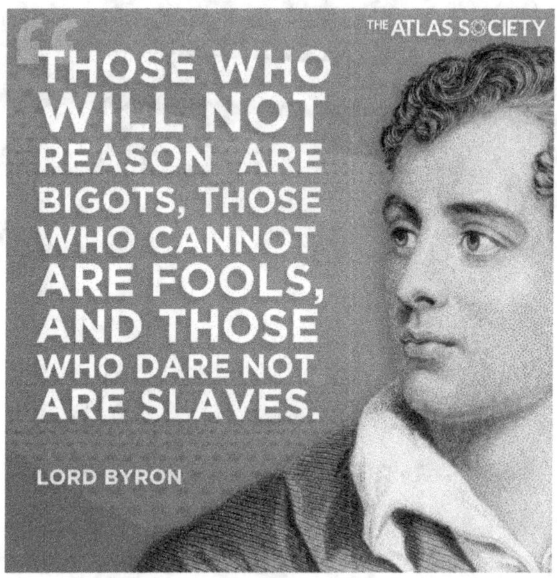

One can argue that this quote's accusatory structure is emotionally delivered, but in no way does it attempt to incite one to political action, take political sides, or defend a political ethic. There is no attempt to sway a vote or to incite violence. Like this book, it simply suggests that a rational attitude works to one's favor in making important decisions more often than does an emotional attitude.

When distant and unfamiliar and complex
things are communicated to great masses
of people, the truth suffers a considerable
and often a radical distortion.
The complex is made over into the simple,
the hypothetical into the dogmatic,
and the relative into an absolute.
— Walter Lippmann (1889–1974)

And, of course:

The Ten Commandments of Logic

1. Thou shalt not attack the person's character, but the argument. *(Ad hominem)*

2. Thou shalt not misrepresent or exaggerate a person's argument in order to make it easier to attack. *(Straw man fallacy)*

3. Thou shalt not use small numbers to represent the all. *(Hasty generalisation)*

4. Thou shalt not argue thy position by assuming one of its premises is true. *(Begging the question)*

5. Thou shalt not claim that because something occured before, it must be the cause. *(Post hoc/False cause)*

6. Thou shalt not reduce the argument down to two possibilities. *(False dichotomy)*

7. Thou shalt not argue that because of our ignorance, a claim must be true or false. *(Ad ignorantum)*

8. Thou shalt not lay the burden of proof onto him that is questioning the claim. *(Burden of proof reversal)*

9. Thou shalt not assume "this" follows "that" when there is no logical connection. *(Non sequitur)*

10. Thou shalt not argue that because a premise is popular, therefore it must be true. *(Bandwagon fallacy)*

Chapter 14.

Post-war Reconstruction

How do you deal with defeated opponents? Some say that once they have fallen, keep them under your boot. Others say that generosity is the answer so that things can get back to at least a peaceful coexistence. What do you say?

If you keep your defeated rivals under your heal, you have become like a tyrant who can brook no dissent. If you give your former rivals a helping hand, you may be helping them create a second opportunity to attack or, at least, undercut you.

Here is an excerpt from a *Wikipedia* article on German reconstruction after World War II:

As agreed at Potsdam, an attempt was made to convert Germany into a pastoral and agricultural nation, allowed only light industry. Many factories were dismantled as reparations, or were simply destroyed (see also the Morgenthau Plan). Millions of German prisoners of war *were for several years used as* forced labor, both by the Western Allies *and the* Soviet Union....

By mid-1947, the success of denazification and the start of the Cold War *had led to a reconsideration of policy, as the Germans were seen as possible allies in the conflict and the dawning realization that the economic recovery of Europe was dependent on the reactivation of German industry. ...*

In 1948, the Deutsche Mark *replaced the* occupation *currency as the currency of the Western occupation zones, leading to their eventual economic recovery.*

In 1947, the Marshall Plan, initially known as the "European Recovery Program" was initiated. In the years 1947–1952, some $13 billion of economic and technical assistance—equivalent to around $140 billion in 2017—were allocated to Western Europe. Despite protests from many beneficiaries, the Marshall Plan, although in the less generous form of loans, was in 1949 extended to also include the newly formed West Germany. In the years 1949–1952, West Germany received loans, which totaled $1.45 billion, equivalent to around $14.5 billion in 2006.

The country subsequently began a slow but

continuous improvement of its standard of living, with the export of local products, a reduction in unemployment, increased food production, and a reduced black market.

By 1950, the UK and France were finally induced to follow the U.S. lead, and stop the dismantling of German heavy industry. The country's economic recovery under the newly formed democratic government was, once it was permitted, swift and effective. …

The reader can use his or her own judgment, of course, but it seems to me that these measures were both punitive and supportive, while remaining aware of the need to adjust to circumstances. Can this post-war reconstruction teach us anything about a post-debate debacle when you can be sure of your victory (or even if you cannot)?

I won. Yay! The opponent has run out of counterarguments and the audience applauds. It's obvious to everyone that you have come out on top in the verbal scuffle. Offer your hand if close enough to do so. Then pick one small point on which you may have agreed and say something like, "I felt you were quite accurate on your point about buying elections. That might be an area in which we can work for a mutual solution."

I thought I won, but who knows for sure? The audience applauds but you are unsure for whom—they may have liked aspects of both side's arguments. Offer your hand if close enough to do so. Then pick one small point on which you may have agreed and say something like, "I felt you were quite accurate on your point about buying elections. That might be an area in which we can work for a mutual solution."

Whoever fights monsters should see to it that, in the process, he does not become a monster.

—Friedrich Nietzsche

Chapter 15.

The Frustration of Inspiration

In the introduction, I explained the combination of influences that conspired to start me writing this book. I had been studying relationships for a long time, was frustrated with how some women dealt with men and how men could never seem to do anything right even if they felt they had done nothing wrong. But I was and am even more frustrated at how political arguments cannot be settled anymore. There is no method of impartial adjudication. Since so many of us no longer agree on what happened in reality even after an investigation takes place, since so many of us no longer hold rationality as the highest possible arbiter of a point-of-view, since so many of us no longer believe reality is or even can be objective, and since so many of us believe that winning is everything, looking for ways to win that are detached from both reality and rationality seem to be the way to go. As long as emotional arguments incite people to take actions that the purveyors of those arguments desire, as long as people would rather feel than think, as long as they feel morally superior when their emotions are satiated, emotions will be valued more highly than careful thinking.

Emotional pleas may help you recognize a problem. They do not help you confirm that it is, in fact, a problem, nor help you solve the problem if it exists. Unfortunately, emotional pleas can also convince you there is a *big* problem when there may be a small problem. Emotional pleas can convince you that you must *act now*, when you could actually take time to consider your options. Emotional pleas can persuade you that your actions can change the world for the better when, in reality, they may be either ineffective or change the world for the worse.

RATIONALITY IN DEFENSE OF EMOTION

Since each of us has values and since we feel strongly about those values, it is completely understandable that we would also become emotional about achieving or defending those values. Is it not therefore understandable that our emotions would come to the fore when we discuss, debate, or argue those values? Yep, that's a great point. Now ask yourself if the emotions you feel in discussing your values should allow you to dispense with rational arguments *in defense* of those values? If you wish to defend your feelings (and the values at the root of those feelings), would you not wish to have reasons for that defense?

Perhaps, like one of my friends, or like Whoopi Goldberg, you feel that your feelings are sufficient, that if you feel strongly enough, it *must* be right. Okay, but how would you convince me that what you feel is right for *me*? In fact, if you go with *your* feelings, haven't you simply persuaded me that it is valid to go with *mine*? We are both free to have our own opinions, aren't we? But, even if going with our own personal feelings seems fair to you, how do you juxtapose either of our feelings with the actual occurrences of reality? How can you verify the validity of your feelings? Sure, the fact that you feel them is real, but is the reason for feeling them verifiable? If you feel sad because your dog died, but you find he was only sleeping, do you hold on to the sadness despite the reality? Are your emotions more important than objective reality? Was your dog actually dead because you felt sad at his immobile state? Do you believe that whatever you feel can overcome what is real? And yet, when discussions and debates occur without reference to empirical data, knowledge of history, or verifiable predictions for the future, that is precisely what the debaters are expecting—that reality will take a backseat to their emotionally preferred ideal.

After the horrible violence of the First World War, there was a very strong pacifist movement in Europe promulgated and defended by many intelligent people who wanted to believe that if their nation diminished its armament, the more heavily armed nations would perceive no threat and thus would leave them in peace. Meanwhile, Hitler was increasing his nation's armament. The European voices of emotional argumentation indulged in labeling, jumping to extreme conclusions, mind reading, drawing conclusions based on facts that could have other interpretations, and assuming that the opposite parties mean something they may not mean. The emotionally powerful pacifist movement described not Hitler, but those who wanted to bolster their countries' armed forces, as warmongers and people who enjoyed violence, all the while assuming a stance of superior morality.

Some of these pacifists were among the most intelligent public figures of the day, but they were intelligent in their own realms, not necessarily in international relations. Nevertheless, the average person might have thought, "Well, Bertrand Russell is a mathematician and a philosopher. Obviously, if he advocates disarmament and national pacifism, he must be thinking logically." It would be understandable if a citizen believed that Russell and others were using their rational faculties to defend their values. In a way, they were. They fashioned well-written, cleverly worded contentions meant to encourage citizens to embrace the cause of peace. Yet a single semester in a high school with a bully would convince even a person of average intelligence that the weak and inoffensive are not exempt from unprovoked physical violence. In other words, a little empirical evidence can be more valuable than wishful idealism. *Wishful thinking and idealism have their own value, but they are not truth. Intelligence does not necessarily yield rationality. And cleverly constructed defenses of emotional positions do not make those positions relate to objective reality.*

If you are a 27-year-old single woman who has just met a guy you would like to tackle into bed, do you first try to find out something about him? If so, you are using rational judgment to support your emotional desires. If he seems trustworthy and sincere, do you immediately dispense with birth control? No? Then you are using rational judgment in support of your long-term emotional ideals.

If you are excited about going to Brazil on vacation, do you check your bank account first? Do you check your schedule? Do you make a hotel reservation? Do you book a flight and arrange for ground transportation to your hotel? Or is all of that supposed to be arranged by your excitement at your potential vacation?

If you want that new 65" smart TV for your living room so you can sit in comfort with your boyfriend watching reruns of *Sex in the City*, would you cancel next year's Brazilian vacation or would you delay buying the new leather reclining loveseat in order to afford the TV? Not being able to have all three is facing reality. Planning to eventually be able to afford all three is applying rationality in support of your emotions.

RATIONALIZATION IN DEFENSE OF EMOTION AIN'T THE SAME

If you've have decided that since you are under-paid, and since the business you work for is making a lot of moolah, you are thus completely justified in lifting computer ink, paper, and disks from your job, you have used your disappointment at your paycheck (emotion) to justify your stealing from your place of work. *Rationalizing* your emotional decision is not the same as reasonably justifying the positions you feel strongly about. Rationalizing is not being rational; rather, it is a way to emotionally abduct your reasoning ability.

YOU CAN DISAGREE EVEN IF BOTH USE RATIONALITY TO SUPPORT EMOTION

In the latter part of the twentieth century, one of the hot-button issues was abortion and only a little less hot, but nonetheless on-the-button, was the issue of capital punishment. Not surprisingly, the stances divided into Left and Right positions. However in those days, both sides at least attempted to defend their emotional positions with rational arguments.

The Left stood for Roe v. Wade, allowing early abortions so that having to raise an unwanted child would not ruin an unmarried woman's life (and perhaps the child's, as well). The Right claimed that all abortion was murder masquerading as healthcare or women's rights.

The Left hated the idea of capital punishment, thinking it "cruel and unusual", while the Right argued that people who commit egregious crimes should suffer capital punishment rather than live at state expense for the rest of their lives. The Left cared about the convicted felon and his family while The Right cared about the forgotten victims of the crime and their families. The Left argued that killing the felon would not undue the crime while The Right argued that executing the felon would serve as a warning to others not to commit felonious acts.

The Right reasoned that the Left was hypocritical since it was unwilling to execute a guilty party via capital punishment but was willing to terminate the life of an innocent party via abortion. The Left reasoned that the Right was hypocritical since it did not care if young women were overburdened with motherhood before they were ready while being overly concerned with the state's expenses for feeding and housing a criminal's during a life sentence.

Each side balanced an emotional appeal with reasoning, given that neither the long-term effects of easy access to abortion nor the alleged deterrents of capital punishment could be known at the time. Without making a formal agreement to wait for more facts, the disagreement was, in essence, put on hold. Regardless of where you stand on these issues, you can see that in those days the emotions were backed up with enough reasoning so that a test could be designed for future judgment. To see which side you favor, it might help to look up the statistics for abortions of unwed mothers from 1970 to the present and for capital punishment during the same period.

A HOT WAR MEETS A COLD WAR IN AN ADVERTISEMENT

When all is said and done, emotionality works. As human beings, we have evolved to react quickly to certain stimuli. Emotions produce the quick judgments and quick reactions needed for survival. In hunter-gatherer days, a slowly considered reaction might mean instant injury or death, so a person, especially a hunter, developed quicker judgments. But a quick judgment does not guarantee that it will be a correct judgment. And the quick judgment of a hunter has to be reinforced by previous experiences, not simply by his emotion. Therefore, careful thinking is also needed for survival, not just for hunters, but especially if you are out in the field picking berries. A berry that thrills the picker with its beauty but has proven to be poisonous will teach the picker that rationally considering a choice is more important than the attractiveness of that choice. However, species-wide detailed reasoning evolved gradually and, in most cases, is not employed as automatically as are emotions. Therefore, although I strongly advocate a cultural return to an emphasis on rationality, I am not idealistic enough to believe that will happen in time for you to win your next political debate.

I have already suggested that fighting emotional fire with emotional fire ends up simply extending the use of emotion. I have also said that fighting fire with cool, rational water is unlikely to convince people who love flames. How about combating the fire of an opponent's emotional argumentation with forest fire tactics? This would be setting counter-fires as well as having cooler flame-retardants at the ready, thus using emotions to counter a debate-opponent's emotions, then dousing the argument with facts.

Here's another way of conceptualizing the forest fire analogy. A full-out hot war has to be fought with a full-out hot war—emotion vs. emotion; however, at the same time, a nation at war will use cold-war tactics to try to win "the hearts and minds" of the opposing nation's people. Propaganda can be a cold-war use of hot emotion backed up by logic. Reason in an emotional framework can be an appeal to "hearts and minds", very much like honest marketing.

Analyze the next few TV commercials you see. You will notice that the advertisement tries to grab you with an image and/or a leading line to make you pay attention. (Images, by the way, are chosen to immediately provoke an emotional response—like suddenly seeing the saber tooth tiger.) "Do you suffer from acid indigestion? Do you have difficulty going to sleep at night, and wake up grumpy with foul breath?" *Well gosh, Maybelle! Let's tune into to this one! This may be the solution I've been waiting for!* Then the ad gives you several product features that back up its claim of offering a solution: (1) it's been tested in three acclaimed labs, (2) it has the active ingredient Bel Chuless that doctors recommend more than any other, and (3) it works in only 9.7 minutes! *Great Maybelle! Sounds like this has a reasonable chance of working!* On top of all that (going back to the emotional), the entire Mexican Olympic Rowing Team swears by it! These advertisements appeal, to one degree or another, to both your heart and your mind.

In contemporary times, emotions are indulged even more frequently and with greater ease than in the past. Consider the frequent enjoyment (for better or for worse) of exotic foods, music, movies, TV, sports, alcohol, drugs, sexual indulgence, etc. None of these are necessary for survival, but certain people use them so liberally that some of them seem indispensable. Thus certain people create a *de facto* addiction to their emotions.

Affluent nations produce more options for self-indulgence because there is more dispensable income. More self-indulgence quickly widens to sharing and wanting others to be able to indulge in "the good things of life". I find it ironic that "the good things of life" are rarely thought to include deeper academic study and concentrated intellectual effort toward producing the industries, businesses, services, technology, products, health practices, and knowledge of human nature that benefit humankind. In the contemporary world (c. 2020 at this writing), it's not that fewer people than in the past find joy in the idea of benefiting others; rather, it's that fewer people find joy in the rational thinking that makes benefiting others possible.

An *emotional* inspiration may inspire the intellectual effort it takes to produce a value that everyone enjoys, but that inspiration is frustrated if the *intellectual* effort is not appreciated or held as an ideal by others who benefit from it. Therefore, in this emotional culture, it is unlikely that verbal appeals to emotions will diminish.

What if, instead, we could simply increase the respect for rationality by little bits, here and there? What if the way to do that were to address the emotions first and then back them with empirical evidence and logical reasoning, like a hot war and a cold war working together?

Example 1. Feeling for Illegals

YOU: I understand your concern with the illegal immigrants at the border. They go through more than a little bit of hell to get here and then in many cases they have to be turned away or detained until judges can hear their cases.

OPPONENT: That's why they sneak in! Who wants to trek northward for a month and then be detained for months before you are then turned away? It's unfair!

YOU: I understand. Imagine how horrible it must be for those who applied legally for citizenship and then have to wait years, in the countries they are trying to leave, before there is an opening. Imagine how unjust it is for a person who did things *legally* to find out that an illegal paid a coyote to skirt our laws and then took a job that he might have had. People who work hard to get here legally should not be treated this way. I also think it is also unfair that coyotes, drug runners, and human traffickers use desperate souls, who want to flee their benighted country, simply to make a profit. Currently, the criminals make money and the immigrants who apply legally are frustrated. As you say, "It's unfair!"

Example 2. Feeling for the Unarmed Perpetrator

OPPONENT: It is unacceptable that police shoot unarmed black men.

YOU: I know. Even if they were in the aftermath of a robbery, you'd think there would be other ways for police to deal with robbers.

OPPONENT: Exactly. The damn cops are racists!

YOU: But the shooting I was thinking about was last week in Detroit. The cop was black and had been fired upon before the perpetrator threw his gun at the cop while charging him.

OPPONENT: Still, that means the civilian had no gun. Black cops can be racists, too. As soon as you put on the blue, they drum racism into you.

YOU: I feel bad for the criminal who did not get his day in court. I also feel bad for the cop who had to do his job, as ugly as it was. But you know, I feel really bad for the Asian owners of the store since this was their fourth robbery in six months, and feel especially bad for the teenaged black clerk whom the perpetrator pistol-whipped. I feel extremely bad for all the customers that depended upon that store since it will now be closing due to too much crime and insufficient numbers of cops to cover the area.

Example 3. Feeling for Innocents Being Shot

OPPONENT: It's always a wonder to me that you are willing to allow so many deaths during school shootings simply because you will not voluntarily give up your obsession with The Second Amendment.

YOU: It's always a wonder to me that you are willing to tolerate gang-related killings in sections of inner cities.

OPPONENT: What does that have to do with school shootings? Innocent kids are killed because people like you love guns.

YOU: Innocent kids are killed because people, quite unlike me, illegally get their hands on guns, as is shown in both the example of the majority of school shootings *and* in the example of gang violence.

OPPONENT: You are making my point. Fewer guns would mean fewer killings in both areas.

YOU: You always want to punish the innocent for the sins of the guilty. Restricting gun ownership for law-abiding citizens has no effect on the majority of innocent deaths that happen in the inner cities. But you never seem to talk about confiscating illegal guns from criminals. Does that mean you are willing to allow inner city kids with illegal guns to keep killing each other as long as those who legally own guns give them up voluntarily?

Design your own advertisement for what you believe in. Use emotion and then back it up with empirical data. If you have only emotion and no empirical evidence, or if you need to cull through the facts to find only the facts you want to display, consider revamping your position. You may find that the results you desire are more attainable in objective reality if you do not satisfy yourself with an unrealistic perfectionism.

Chapter 16.

What If We Don't?

What if there is no cultural change? What if emotional arguments do not diminish in our society and rational arguments do not increase?

Currently, adults use emotional argumentation in political disputes, but the habit will no doubt filter down to college students, high school students, grade school students, and pre-school students, primarily because it will be culturally accepted. I'm not referring here to college students shouting epithets or slogans during demonstrations, but their using emotional tactics in classroom discussions or written assignments.

Ironically, in my opinion, emotional argumentation has also filtered up from children. "Pre-feminist" argumentation works on men because the women that used it were more in touch with their emotions thus consciously or unconsciously had the insight to touch a man's emotions. Both were adults, but one was more skilled at tweaking an emotional nerve or two. But, children of both genders have always used emotion to manipulate their parents, so it is difficult to say if the filtering process goes up, down, or both ways.

In either case, emotional arguments, now so pervasive in modern life, will no doubt become more pervasive if we do not strongly promote rational, evidence-based argumentation as the preferred mode of debate and discussion.

SCHOOLS

Graduate School Theses. Should a dissertation panel judge a graduate thesis by its emotional or its rational persuasiveness? Does the candidate deserve a Master of Arts or a Doctor of Philosophy degree because she can make you feel strongly, or is it because she is contributing a new intellectual perception, detail, or angle of approach to a field of study? Would that new approach to the field of study be more valuable if the candidate made you laugh, cry, feel anger, or feel jealousy? Only if the thesis were a play script or other work of fiction would we accept the ability to manipulate our emotions as relevant. In all other cases, the candidate's talent with words may help the readability of the thesis, but it does not help convince the reader of the theme's validity.

The value of adding knowledge to a field of study is obvious to everyone. Yes, sometimes the added knowledge comes in the form of variations of interpretation, especially in non-scientific fields, but even so, would established professors accept a new interpretation of literature, psychological behavior, or history if there were no sound arguments and accepted facts to back it up?

Ironically, many academics, having earned their PhDs through rational argumentation, give up trying to contribute knowledge to their fields and concentrate on becoming well known. Public notoriety can be completely independent of a teacher's prowess in the classroom, as a researcher, or as a contributor to her field. When the professor is less than stellar in her discipline, notoriety can act as a shield against peer disapproval, as well as a retardant to deeper research. A learned-*sounding* opinion that catches the public's attention may be all that is needed for an academic to be launched into the public eye. Then the "scholar" has a vested interest in using clever wording and contorted arguments to defend her unique opinion, further slipping away from verifiable empirical evidence and rational argumentation.

In a way, this kind of public notoriety is like going over the boss's head to the CEO. The boss cannot challenge the CEO; similarly, colleagues find it difficult to challenge the public.

Undergraduate Final Examinations. "Hello, Professor Hotchins? Yeah, this is N. Tyteld, from your History 103b class. I really think you need to reconsider my grade on the essay exam! I am in danger of not qualifying for the soccer team, so just a B- would be enough to put me over. What do you mean I was lucky to get a D? My parents paid for these classes! The exam was silly and besides you know the soccer team needs its best center forward on the field all the time. If I don't get a B- from you, you'll be the reason we lose the playoffs! If I don't get at least a B-, I'll make sure no one gives you higher than a D in your annual student evaluation."

You may feel that this scenario is impossible. You certainly would not have dared challenge Professor Hotchins to reconsider your grade without first having marshalled some very good arguments in your own favor. Unless you had been ill or your mother had just died, you would not plea, but instead would have supplied evidence and sound reasoning while arguing the merits of the concepts that you had presented on the essay exam.

And yet phone calls like this have been made to professors, partially because professors know they need to serve the student as a consumer and partially because the student will always find it easier to plea then to reason. (See Tom Nichol's book *The Death of Expertise*.)

High School Class Participation. In some high school classes, teachers calculate a portion of the grade based on classroom participation. Teachers have always thought it valuable that students learn to shed their fear of public speaking, learn to articulate properly, show that they can draw on their knowledge somewhat extemporaneously, and make a cogent argument, rather than simply turn in reports, the source of which can be suspect. A high school student I knew—I'll call her Julia—was able to "earn" a good grade for class participation simply by challenging whatever a fellow student posited as a point of view. Johnny would say, "It seems to me that in *The Republic*, Plato is hypothesizing an ideal society that could, in fact, be tried in a tightly overseen nation, but is unlikely to work in a nation that values personal freedom." To this, Julia would look pensive and chime in, "Or *could* it?" at which point another more astute student would take up her cause and argue for the strict structures seen in *The Republic*. Then, by readily agreeing with the more astute student, Julia was able to create the perception that that student's ideas had been her own, implying, "Yes, precisely as I would have stated it."

Julia was not using emotional argumentation, but she was doing her best to avoid the hard work of thinking about what she had read, reflecting on it, coming to a thesis, and making a rationally defensible argument.

Grade School. When children are too young to have experience forming rational arguments and too young to use their minds to create clever emotional appeals, they can and do simply "argue" with adults by force of their own emotions.

I was operating a basic martial arts class as part of a Montessori school's athletic program. Having already taught basics to the fifth and sixth grade students for two sessions, I broke them into teams to see which group of kids remembered the movements the best. This would give them an incentive to pay closer attention to what I taught and would give them a team spirit that is usually absent from martial arts training.

"Who wants to be a captain? Okay, you five step forward. Pick a number from 1 to 100. Whoever guesses the closest to the number in my head are the team captains." No problem there. Bobby and Mary got the closest numbers.

"Okay, now go to each side of the room make up a name for your team." Again, no problem: Bobby's would be The Flaming Dragons and Mary's would be The Ultimate Champions. "Okay, Dragon captain, your number was the closer of the two, so you get first pick of the other students." Great! The kids were really getting excited about the contest. After three rounds of picks, Bobby chose Percy. I motioned Percy to walk to the opposite side of the room to join The Flaming Dragons.

"I don't wanna be on that team."

"But, Percy, you were just chosen."

"I don't wanna be on that team."

I did not know if his resistance was because of the team captain, the other members whom had already been chosen, the team name, the physical side of the room, or someone on the other team that Percy wanted to be with. "But, Percy, *why* don't you want to be on that team?" I figured I could meet him halfway and have mid-season player trades or switch sides of the room in mid-game.

"I just don't wanna."

"Well, sorry, you can either be on that team or sit out and watch the others."

"No! I wanna be on *this* team," he said pointing to The Ultimate Champions.

The episode ended with my escorting Percy to the Headmaster's office, which was next to the recreation room.

Percy did not feel obliged to give me either a rational or an emotional reason for his resistance, so I could not solve his problem or even compromise. His petulant position was "my way no matter what". Why? "Because I *want* it!"

Tom Nichols writes in *The Death of Expertise*: "When feelings matter more than rationality or facts, education is a doomed enterprise. Emotion is an unassailable defense against expertise, a moat of anger and resentment in which reason and knowledge quickly drown. And when students learn that emotion trumps everything else, it is a lesson they will take with them for the rest of their lives."

THE WORK PLACE

Solving the problem. In every line of employment, problems have to be solved. Sometimes they are as simple as, "Boss, this meat doesn't look good. I don't think I should put it on the grill." Sometimes they are as complicated as, "Sir, Southern Midco Supplies just called. It did not receive its shipment of astro-plungers to make their hover-pod component of our G-20 Personal Goblin Flyer. The Pentagon is expecting our shipment Monday and since we have already postponed delivery twice, if we do so again, we will lose the contract." Threats, pleas, or petulant pouting will not solve work place problems like these.

Imagine that Imogen has secured a job as a commercial artist working for Creative Creations for Commerce. She is assigned to visually create the individual pages of customers' websites before those images are passed on to the tech department where the images are digitized, converted to jpg format, and then used as a template for setting up the links and subpages that the customer has requested. Customer Steward D. Baker, who sells auto literature and hard-to-get parts for old Chryslers, wants specialty pages for every kind of part from the 1930s onward. Imogen, who once owned a 2004 Plymouth, balks at creating those pages since she thinks that Chrysler Corp. did not treat her well when her car developed problems after only 13 months on the road. She feels that it is an immoral company and she will not have anything to do with it.

"Okay," says her boss, "but you must realize that Mr. Baker is dealing in older Chryslers and is trying to help people who have collected classic Chryslers. He doesn't deal in Plymouths and he doesn't work for Chrysler Corporation."

But no, Imogen insists, she will not comply. Her ethical stance is more important to her than any job that would take money from a business that makes money from a product produced by an unethical corporation. She is offended that she has been asked to indirectly benefit a corporation (so she says) that she feels has treated her poorly.

"But Imogen, you can trace back any offense, imagined or real, to a root of an origin of a derivation of a cause! That means you'll constantly be offended and no work will get done."

"Maybe," says Imogen, "but I will be standing for moral correctness!"

"Sorry, Imogen, your work is good, but I need someone who will do the job. I'll tell payroll to pay you for the rest of the day, but as of right now, you're fired."

SPORTING CONTESTS

Would you watch a football game if you knew that the emotion you felt when the star quarterback throws a Hail Mary pass for the winning touchdown with half a second left on the clock could be countered by the other teams squad of cheerleaders crying into the cameras? "How unfair it is that your team has a quarterback with such a good arm while our team never seems to make the playoffs!" they say. No? You wouldn't watch such a game? But c'mon! That team never wins.

The lowest ranked teams get earliest pick in the college player draft in attempt to allow all teams accessibility to player talent, but still that team doesn't seem to win! It's just not fair! It must be because of some systemic bias and the overwhelming popularity of the other team's great quarterback. Nevertheless, please come watch the games, especially the games in which those cheerleaders can plead for equality for their losing team! You might leave unsatisfied with the skills of the football players, but you will be greatly satisfied with the emotional argumentation skills of their cheerleaders.

COURTS

"Your honor, although my client, a teacher in city's Middle School #3, admits to setting fire to several businesses in the downtown area, the leaders of the peaceful protests against systemic economic aggression told him that this was the virtuous thing to do. He was merely following the heightened enthusiasm of the crowd and should not be punished for his youthful indiscretions."

GAME SHOWS

This online cartoon sums up the argument:

EMOTION CONFUSED WITH MORALITY

"Fairness" and "equality" are hot-button words because they carry an ethical implication. If an emotional argument uses "fairness" or "equality" as part of the presentation, people will be ready to assume that those emotional arguments are justified, as if simply asserting that the opposition is unfair or promotes inequality makes the assertion true.

Because both words are linked to ethical principles, it is easy to get them confused. Fairness is "going by the rules" while Equality can have two meanings: (1) being treated the same way everyone else is, according to predetermined rules (i.e. Fairness), or (2) having identical characteristics or outcomes (Equity of Results). When we see blatant cheating in any facet of life, we respond with indignity and anger. So, if a person argues with an air of indignity and anger, it seems to enhance the credibility of his unfairness or inequality claims. In contradistinction, many people read a calm disposition while defending one's position rationally as being indifferent or inauthentic.

A moment's reflection will convince you that exhibiting emotion does not make you accurate nor does a calm demeanor make you uncaring. Emotion is no more equated with morality as acting moral is equated with being accurate.

EMOTIONAL ARGUMENTS IN LIEU OF INTELLECTUAL ARGUMENTS

Often in political arguments, emotion is about demanding the ideal; rationality is figuring out how to approach the ideal. Emotion assumes everyone can be happy and thus those who stand in the way of that ideal want people to be unhappy. However, Tony Robbins tells us that happiness comes from progress, not perfection. Progress is applying one's rational mind to improvement.

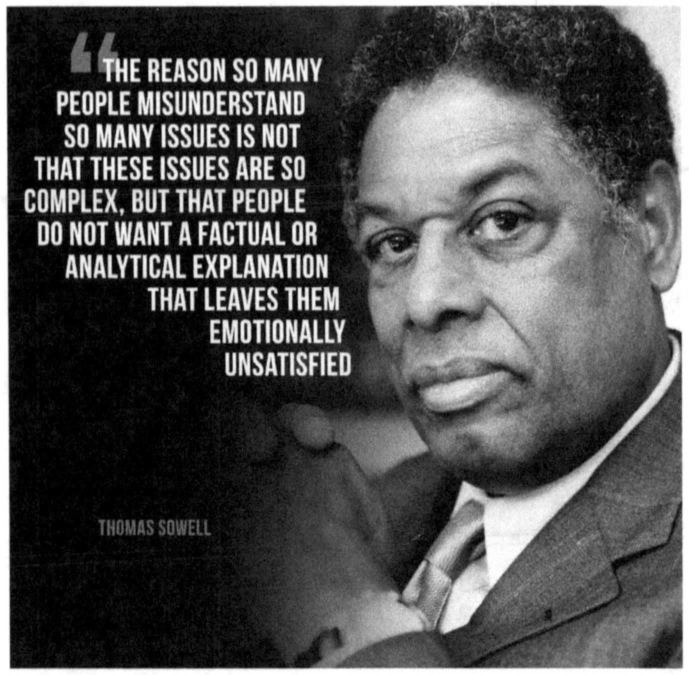

Epilogue

Right or Left?

Both sides of the political aisle are guilty of assuming "truths" about the other side. In each case, their assumptions are based on evidence, which is then exaggerated out of proportion, unless of course, the assumptions reference only the extremes of each party. The average, every day Liberal claims a Left affiliation mainly because he/she absolutely does not want to be a Conservative. Why? Here is a meme that exemplifies what the Left often assumes about the Right. At first glance, the average moderate Liberal will instantly agree, forgetting that every quality can be quantified and thus any quality can be made to look appalling in its extreme, just as a pat on the back is good but a whack on the back of the head is bad. In other words, this meme assumes an extreme position and thus takes advantage of confirmation bias.

Anyone can see the analogy on the surface. However, measuring the degree of each position changes the picture. Fundamental to the success of the meme is that the reader will assume that Muslims, Isis, and Sharia Law are all one unit—an assumption that is precisely what the Left claims to reject.

First, all Conservatives are not religious and all religious people are not Conservative. The average Conservative does not want his religion to control the government; rather, he sees the values of the government as already based on broad Judeo-Christian values and thus does not want to see those values eliminated from the culture.

Second, Conservative *Christians* (but not necessarily Libertarians, Objectivists, or other non-Christians on the Right) would indeed prefer that a prayer start the day in school and in congress, but that 30-second prayer is nothing like the extent that Muslims pray in their schools, which conflate education and religion.

Third, "100% focused on wars" is an attempt at mind reading and has no empirical evidence to back it up. Traditionally, Conservatives want a larger, stronger army than do Liberals, but that hardly means focusing on wars. It ignores wars fought under Democratic/Liberal administrations (most notably WWII and Vietnam) and does not consider which wars the country may have preferred to fight, given the alternative. The unstated implication is that since no war is a good war, all wars are necessary wars, something that is plainly wrong if you accept self-defense as both a human and also a national right.

Fourth, Conservatives are not against women's rights at all, although they are against abortion on demand and state-funded abortion. In contradistinction, the record of women's rights in Islamic states usually is appalling by Western standards.

Fifth, Rupert Murdoch *does* own Fox News, and Saudi Prince Alwaleed bin Talal owns a minor share (6.6%) of it. Murdoch's having an interest in a new Middle Eastern TV station is a more complicated issue. The prince planned to launch a new Arabic television news channel in partnership with Rupert Murdoch as an alternative to al-Jazeera. The prince named the Saudi journalist Jamal Khashoggi as chief of the new network, before Khashoggi's untimely murder.

Sixth, "political religious leaders are filthy rich" is one of those non-arguments that means nothing in itself, but is meant to produce an emotional reaction. Nothing is mentioned of liberal business owners that are "filthy" rich. "Filthy", in my opinion, always seems to apply to the riches of those with whom you disagree.

And seventh, Conservatives *do* oppose sex education in public schools because they feel that parents should introduce that subject to their children; however, Conservatives do not oppose contraceptives, although they oppose distributing them in public schools. And finally, Christian Conservatives may argue that homosexuality is a choice and therefore a sin; however, non-Christian Conservatives (Libertarians, Tea-partiers, etc.) lean strongly toward the live-

and-let-live philosophy. Christian Conservatives *did* oppose homosexual marriage, but once the Supreme Court ruled it legal, they have, for the most part, reverted to the live-and-let-live philosophy. In contradistinction, many Islamic states persecute and execute homosexuals.

Similarly, those who consider themselves Conservatives often are so situated because they do not want to be Liberals. Why? Here is a meme that explains what the Right assumes true of the Left.

Certainly it is true that since Truman and Kennedy, the Democratic Party has gone further to the Left, but so has the Republican Party. Where Liberals were criticized at one time for constantly growing the government, now both sides contribute to that growth.

First, few, if any, everyday Liberals support anarchism, domestic terrorism, or Satanism. Liberals do defend Atheists, who have the right to their beliefs, as does any religious citizen.

Second, when asked about details of the Marxism or Socialism that some Liberals may support, their descriptions of those systems sounds more like the Scandinavian high-tax/high-service market economies than true Marxism.

Third, few Liberals would consider themselves anti-American, however they do concentrate on the perceived flaws of U.S. government policies and U.S. culture, and seldom give them credit for their successes.

Fourth, Liberals *are* more likely to be idealists and therefore more likely to accept Globalism in lieu of Americanism.

Fifth, certainly most Liberals would deplore Fascism, thinking it within the purview of the Right, however they do tend to ignore Fascistic tactics when perpetrated by Leftist demonstrators that become rioters. In fact, when

Leftist causes become hijacked by Marxists, terrorists, or Fascists, most Liberals do not support the tactics, but do not speak out against them, either.

Note that both graphic memes use partial facts in order to elicit an emotional response.

Because of some the fictitious examples I use in this book, many people will figure that I am ensconced on the Right side of the political aisle with just enough of a nod to Left-leaning ideas to make me look Centrist. Nah. I wish it were that simple, but it isn't. I think both sides of the aisle have lost their ways, but currently (as of 2020) I think that the Left tends to use emotional arguments in discussions and debates more frequently than the Right. (Both sides use emotion when employing memes.) The Left, with its tendency to try new things, has usually led the way in political innovation either in policy or in campaigning. The Right, with its tendency to maintain the status quo, has usually reacted to whatever the Left has tried. In this way the Right is literally "reactionary" (even when it does not oppose liberalization or reform, as the Left defines "reactionary").

I often cringe at the Right's fecklessness, feeling that they should be the ones upholding the Classical Jeffersonian Liberalism to which they once aspired, and I regularly become incensed at the Left's employing political dirty tricks, then trying to disguise them using hot-button words to prompt an emotional response. Thus, riots become *demonstrations*, the Founding Fathers become aristocratic *racists*, restrictions on bathroom use violate *civil rights*, etc.

I believe that the circular gauge used in today's world to reference Left and Right has become useless and in many cases flat out inaccurate. The following is a graphic example of that circular scale. Imagine an invisible arrow pinned to the center of the dial and pointing to twelve. As it rotates to the right (clockwise), it approaches Fascism. As the invisible arrow goes to the left (counterclockwise), it approaches Communism. The implications of the dial are that an extreme form of both Leftism and Rightism ends up in some sort of Statism—government control.

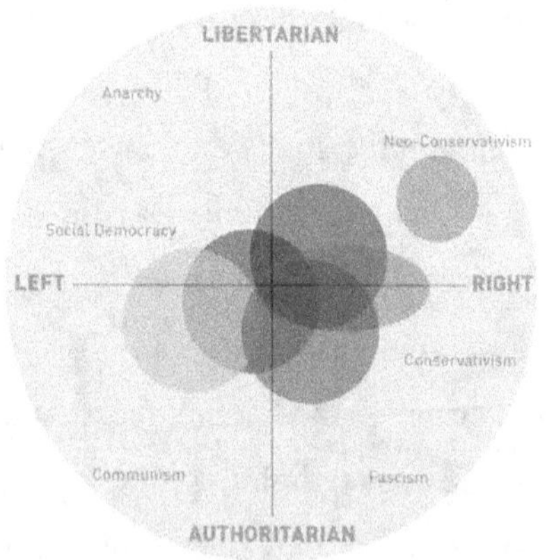

(Source: Political spectrum of Toronto's Mayor's race, January, 2010)

A linear form of the above gauge would be something like this:

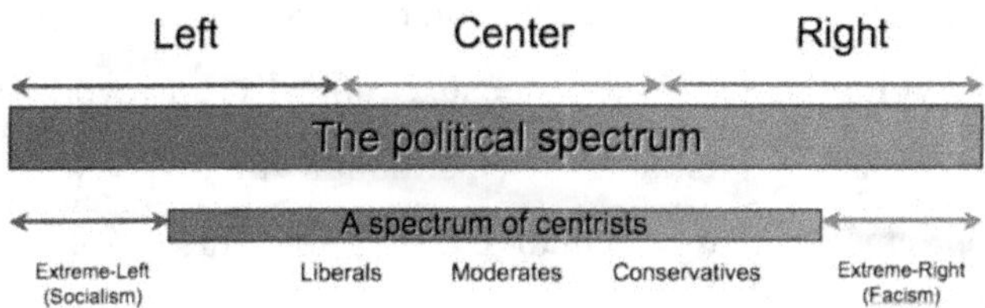

I prefer an older scale, one that was used during the founding of the USA, as shown here:

Whether or not you agree with the 2011 placement of the American Left or the placement of Conservatives, for example, I would suggest that this scale is more accurate in understanding the Left and the Right in philosophical terms. The founders wanted a Center-Right government (as shown on this scale) and would have put any sort of Statism/Authoritarianism (whether Fascism, Nazism, Socialism, Communism, or dictatorship) on the far left and anarchy on the far right. Who is more emotionally driven than anarchists that feel free to indulge themselves and refuse to listen to rational arguments about self-control? In this older scale, it is the Right, not the Left, which tends to indulge its emotions: the more anarchistic a person becomes, the less he/she is willing to discuss and debate. Ironically, however, that suggests that Rightist-anarchists, although emotional, would not use emotional argumentative tactics since they would not argue at all.

Having stated my preference for this version of the political scale, let me hasten to add that reality seldom cooperates in dividing itself into a neat categories, philosophies, or political sides. At this writing (mid-2020), the USA is experiencing riots and looting and demands for fewer police—a clearly anarchistic position, and yet it is sponsored by self-admitted Marxist organizations, almost as if the authoritarian extreme Left is using the anarchistic extreme Right (using the above scale) to tear down a culture for which the replacement will clearly be one the Far Left prefers, while hiding its authoritarian nature under flags of Liberty and Equality.

Because these political categories are so easily misunderstood and sometimes willfully misused, I find it more productive that people who wish to have an honest and open interchange or debate, discuss *values* rather than positions.

When I discuss issues with friends who consider themselves on the Right, I find that they are always well informed about the current Right-speak talking points and also informed about the current Left-speak talking points. I suspect this is because people on the Right feel they have to be "reactive" to the cultural pressure coming from institutions that are currently dominated by the Left (see Tim Grossclose's *Left Turn*). However, when I discuss issues with friends who consider themselves on the Left, I find that they are always well informed about the current Left-speak talking points, but seldom informed about the current Right-speak talking points. Recognizing that this could relate only to my specific group of friends, I have tried to watch TV discussion panel shows in order to get the give-and-take that I used to get by watching *Meet the Press*, *Face the Nation*, and *Firing Line* in the 1960s, and *The McLaughlin Group* in the 1980s. But, in the current political atmosphere, each panel tends to favor the Left or the Right and either ignores or has only a token representative of the other side.

Then I realized that people entrenched in their camps seldom visit the camp over the hill, so I must have been going about making a rational point to friends incorrectly. It was not because I wasn't making sense, but because entrenched populations, if separated long enough, actually speak a different dialect.

I remember my dad explaining to me what his

father had explained to him: that back in Italy, one group of people would speak Italian in a certain way while "on the other side of the hill", another group spoke that same language another way. He explained that these were "dialects". People from each group could converse with the other if they cared to, but sometimes they had to clarify what they meant. Sometimes, this would be complicated by different references and preferences. If fishermen interacted with farmers or farmers interacted with hunters, their commonly used terms and their lifestyles would influence their preferences even though their generic values (freedom to support themselves, ownership rights, freedom to market their goods, etc.) might be the same. Imagine if they did not regularly interact. Soon the multidimensional labors of the fishermen would seem strange to the simpler and more repetitive labor of the farmer. Similarly, the early rising farmer's predictable labor would seem nonsensical to the hunter's follow-the-prey labor—even though each shared the value of wanting to provide sustenance for their families.

Now, when I talk to friends who have different political points of view, instead of asking what they think about a policy or a political proposal, I ask what is of prime importance to them. That which is of prime importance is a high value and something they can feel passionate (emotional) about. To coax them toward the rational, I then ask what practical steps they, their party, or their government should take to make that value come to fruition.

Bibliography

The problem isn't that Johnny can't read. The problem isn't even that Johnny can't think. The problem is that Johnny doesn't know what thinking is; he confuses it with feeling.

—Thomas Sowell

AUDIO

Sowell, Thomas, *Intellectuals and Society*, audio edition, Blackstone Audio, Inc., 2009

BOOKS

Annesi, Tony, *10 Guideline Principles*, Amazon & B&N, 2019
—, *10 Common Values*, Amazon & B&N, 2019
—, *Your Ethics Are Immoral*, Amazon & B&N, 2020
Burg, Bob, *Adversaries into Allies*, Portfolio/Penguin, 2013
Freedman, David, *Wrong*, Little, Brown and Company, 2010
Grossclose, Tim, *Left Turn*, St. Martin's Press, 2011
Haidt, Jonathan, *The Righteous Mind*, First vintage Book Edition, 2012
Huxley, Aldous, *Brave New World*, Bantam Edition, 1960
Nichols, Dan, *The Death of Expertise*, Oxford University Press, 2019
Sterling, A. Justin, *What Really Works with Men*, Warner Books, Inc., 1992

WEBSITES

Dhar, Julia: *https://www.ted.com/talks/julia_dhar_how_to_disagree_productively_and_find_common_ground*

Headlee, Celeste: https://www.ted.com/talks/celeste_headlee_10_ways_to_have_a_better_conversation

Liveabout: https://www.Liveabout.com

NPR.org

O'Reilly, Bill & Whoopi Goldberg: *https://www.foxnews.com/story/whoopi-goldberg-on-hollywood-politics*

Wikipedia: *https://en.wikipedia.org/wiki/Shooting_of_Michael_Brown*

----- *https://en.wikipedia.org/wiki/Reconstruction_of_Germany*

Addenda

This Just In

While proofreading this book for what I had hope to be the final time (believe me, one never knows how many times one will have to proofread his own work), I received a call from a lawyer friend and we discussed everyday items like her workload and my having to hire someone to replace parts of my central air conditioning unit, etc. We disagree about politics so we avoid that subject as a matter of course. She said she was worried about going to New York during the CoVid-19 crisis, and I mentioned that New York was doing well now, with cases dropping. Then she asked me the question she seemed to ask every other time we talked, "Your not worried about this, are you?"

"Not especially," I said, "It's a real virus, but I think it has been way overblown. And worse, you don't know where you can find accurate information about masks, distancing, etc. The W.H.O. says one thing, then the C.D.C. says another, then they seem to change their opinions."

"Well, I get my information from Johns Hopkins. I don't think they have a political axe to grind."

"Great," I said, "If you have found a trustworthy source for information, that's great."

"But don't you think it [CoVid] is dangerous?"

"It's not that," I said. "My problem is the illogic of public officials that compel us to do this, that, or the other thing. I understood the two-week shutdown so that hospital capacity would not be overwhelmed. We did that. Hospitals handled the load. Then they closed 'unessential' businesses. Then there was the debate about masks. Okay, let's assume masks are a good idea. Let's further assume that even though masks work to prevent the spread of the virus, keeping 6 feet between you and the next guy is an added measure of protection. If these things are true, why shut down businesses? And why is it that the supermarket can open with customers wearing masks and distancing, but the mom and pop variety store cannot? If masks and distancing work, why don't they work in all sorts of stores? Every store can mark off their floors like the supermarket or BJ's does. Shutting down businesses does not make logical sense."

"Well, you know, we are still learning about the virus. This caught everyone by surprise."

"That's not my point. I simply want those in charge to not be self-contradictory. It's bad enough that you can't trust medical authorities since they seem to disagree, but if we have to obey local ordinances, they can at least not be self-contradictory. It's irrational. If one business can open, so can another."

She brought up a governor she felt was doing a good job and I agreed with her but took exception to his requiring nursing homes to admit CoVid patients, resulting in the death of thousands.

"Oh, but that happened in several places," she said.

I held my breath to eschew offering the logical retort of "so how does that make it right?" but I wanted to avoid getting too political. Instead, I repeated that I disagreed with the overall shutdown of the economy, even when governors were "doing a good job", and that I wanted more definitive statements of where, when, and even if civilian masks work.

"But this is a pandemic! Aren't you concerned?"

"Last I looked, the world is 56 million cases short of the Swine Flu epidemic of 2009 during which there were no masks and no shutdowns."

She reiterated her thesis that we are learning and adapting as we go and then claimed that even the president was adjusting his stance. Then she could not help herself from going "political". "Of course, his adjustment is political. He's doing that because he's afraid he'll lose voters…."

I raised my voice, "If you start getting political, you'll lose. Mayors and governors are using their powers to prevent people from going to church or assembling for a funeral, but protests are okay."

Upset at my raising my voice, she said, "You can do all the research you want. I think I'm an intelligent woman. If someone doesn't agree with you, you browbeat them! You are getting hysterical! This conversation's over!"

I'll leave it to the reader to analyze the emotional and rational parts of the conversation and to recognize any argumentation tactics that might have been used.

About the Author

Tony Annesi's writing started with poetry and short fiction (the first stories of *1969: Loss of Innocence* were drafted in 1969) and then followed his martial arts career with columns for INSIDE KARATE MAGAZINE (Tales of the Dojo and The Dojo Files) and articles for MARTIAL ARTS MASTERS, SELF-DEFENSE WORLD, INSIDE KUNG-FU, THE INTERNATIONAL FIGHTER, and BLACK BELT. He has authored *Cracking the Kata Code, The Road to Mastery, Principles of Advanced Budo, Sudden Attack Defense, Elevated Elementals, Comparative Aiki in Action,* and several volumes of essays called *Sunday with Sensei's Journal.*

In 2015, after 12 years of work, Tony completed a fantasy novel trilogy entitled *The Shangrilla Artifacts*. In 2018, he published the sequel, *An Atlantis of One.*

His books of social commentary include *10 Guideline Principles: Finding One's Way in a Messy World, 10 Common Value to Unify a Contentious Culture,* and *Your Ethics Are Immoral.*

10 GUIDELINE PRINCIPLES

The old saying goes: "If you don't stand for something, you'll fall for anything." Unfortunately, in today's messy world, the thing you stand for may be the very thing you have fallen for. Sometimes you need an owner's manual, sometimes a compass, sometimes you need a few suggestions that worked for somebody else. The world no longer functions by the conventions and unwritten rules with which many of us grew up. Although the old guidelines may still work, we may have to see them in new ways. Here's what has worked for me. I hope something similar helps you pass through the fire swamps modern life presents.

10 COMMON VALUES

What if the Left and the Right actually shared fundamental ideas and differed only in preferred implementation?

What if the circular scale we have been using to gauge points of view were really a straight line?

What if we had a set of simple values to rally around?

And what if you could find out all about how people could get together again in the pages of one little book?

YOUR ETHICS ARE IMMORAL

Most of us try to act ethically, drawing our standards from our social upbringing (The Ethic of Community), from our religions (The Ethic of Divinity), or from our own personal reasoning (The Ethic of Autonomy), but we don't always agree on what's right. In this pithy book that combines social commentary with both philosophy and psychology, Tony Annesi suggests that even if we cannot always bridge the gaps between our ethics, we can use both reason and rational self-interest to evaluate them.

PETULANT

Upset women have often been able to disarm men using emotional arguments. Men then incorrectly assume women incapable of rationality—an undeniably sexist attitude. Currently, however, men as well as women use emotional arguments to disarm their political opponents, setting a dangerous precedent by allowing empirical data and rationality to seem ineffectual, thus making passion rather than reason the ultimate arbiter of a dispute.